Laugh Without Prejudice

Pat Ingoldsby

Killeen

How lovely to meet Brona! Lots of love, from [signature]

HOWTH 13/11/97

First published
in November1996 by
Killeen Books,
Killeen,
Blackrock Village,
Cork City,
Ireland

Acknowledgements are due to *In Dublin, The Evening Press* and *Sunday Miscellany* where most of this book first appeared.

ISBN 1-873548-37-0

This book is printed in Dublin by Colour Books on acid free Munken paper. Acid free paper will not discolour or grow brittle with age.

Typeset by the publishers
Colour separations by Upper Case Ltd. Cork
Cover Photo: Liz Twomey

Dedication

With much love to you right now…that's right…to you…reading this…now…at this moment…lovely…and there's not a thing they can do about it!

Contents

A Present To Myself

I have decided to slow myself down significantly this year. No more crazy rushing or panicking or hyper-active pressure. I've made a start by doing a very simple calculation. 365 days during which I shall be awake for approximately sixteen hours each day. That works out as 350,400 minutes. No matter which way you look at it that is a super-abundance of time. It's the perfect answer to give to the negative voices inside my head. "No Pat... you couldn't possibly write a new play this year... that sort of thing takes AGES!" But I've got ages, thank you very much... I've got 350,400 magnificent gilt edged minutes... I'll work it all out for you in seconds if you like.

With so much time on my side this year I'm going to really experience and taste and feel every single thing that I do.

No more hurried breakfasts or gobbled dinners with one eye on my food and the other on the clock. This year it's going to be: "Good morning toast — I now propose to cover you very slowly with delicious apple jelly and then I'm going to consciously enjoy every lazy relaxed chew."

From now on I'm going to concentrate on only being as busy as I choose to be. The generally accepted consensus seems to be that unless you are rushed off your feet, up to your eyes and put to the pin of your collar, there is something very wrong with your life. Frantic, wild-eyed people keep dashing up to me and asking: "Are they keeping you busy?"... or "Busy are we?" They ask the question with manic high-energy and are only programmed to respond to a "Yes, thank God" answer with "That's a good complaint!"

I never want to be so busy anymore that I don't notice morning rain on cobwebs, a snail wandering up the side of my house and heading towards the roof, a baby trying to catch its own toes. This year, armed with my bounty of over 350 thousand minutes I'm going to pause and say: "Good morning spider, thank you for weaving such silver perfection outside my front door. Hello there snail... I hope you enjoy the view when you get to the top. If you look over towards the two big red chimneys you should be able to see Dun Laoghaire from here."

It's been a long time now since I climbed a tree... so I'm going to. I'm going to get the 42 bus out to the woodlands in Malahide and find a nice easy one. When I get to the top I'm going to stay there for a while and listen and I'm not coming down again until I hear a seagull scream.

It's been many years now since I rolled down a hill... so I'm going to. I'm going to put on some old clothes and get a bus out to Bushy Park because my sister tells me there are some brilliant hills out there... she has actually tested them.

I've made a list of all my 'It's been a long times' and I'm going to have great fun doing them all again... once or twice or even three times. I'm going to hold a shell up to my ear and listen to the ocean, reach through the autumn leaves and kick them high up into the air, buy a quarter pound of clove sweets and really take my time over each one. I'm going to fly a coloured kite on

Dollymount Strand and if anyone asks me for a go I might let them hold the string for a while but not for too long. I'm going to build sandcastles and stick a white feather into the top of each one, dig a tunnel and watch the sea filling it up, press the little bubbles on seaweed and hear them going pop, stand on my head and see if the money falls out of my pockets.... I've got so many exciting 'It's been a long times' on my list and I've got loads of glorious time in which to do them all again.

I read last year in the Farming Supplement of a daily paper that there are 1.4 million pigs in Ireland. I can't remember when I last saw one so I'm going to... I'm going to find myself a farm this year and I'm going to see a pig... if the farmer lets me I'm also going to hold a tiny chicken in my hand, milk a cow, pet a donkey and actually watch a cockerel doing his 'Cock-a-doodle-do'. That is something I have never seen. I suspect that they only ever do it when nobody is looking so I'm going to cover my eyes and pretend.

I signed a receipt on the first day of this year... "Received with thanks... the gift of 350,400 minutes." Now I'

m going to live them.

Hats Off!

I was sitting high up in the visitors' gallery in Dail Eireann. It was my very first time. I was being extra-careful not to make any sudden moves because I didn't want to distract anybody or put them off in the middle of their speech.

The whole viewing area is glassed-in which is fair enough. I'm sure the last thing they want is well-meaning visitors flicking Polo Mints down to their favourite politicians. We can do without that sort of carry-on. A sign on the wall warns you: "no applause". It was certainly the furthest thing from my mind. Unless somebody sprang to their feet down below and launched into "The Rocky Road to Dublin" on a twelve-string banjo I had no intention of clapping anyone.

An usher in a dark uniform tapped me discreetly on the shoulder. "Excuse me," he said. "Would you mind taking off your hat?" There was nobody sitting behind me so I knew that I wasn't blocking anyone's view. So I looked down towards the floor of the house. None of the T.D.s was pointing up in my direction and shaking his fist so I knew it wasn't any of them.

"The Leas Ceann Comhairle has requested that you remove it," he explained. I was dying to know how the usher had received the message. I hadn't seen the Leas Ceann Comhairle whispering to anyone underneath his desk. He certainly hadn't clanged his bell and announced — "Visitor Ingoldsby will take off his hat or leave the house."

A note concerning me and my hat had become an integral part of government proceedings. I felt deeply honoured. It's not every day you are asked to take off your hat by a man who has got the power to ring his bell and send highly-respected T.D.s off to bed without any supper.

I took it off and by God I was proud to do it. If my headgear impinges in any way upon the smooth functioning of government I shall not be found wanting. I will whip it off and in so doing, keep parliamentary democracy on the rails.

I asked the usher if I could have the note. I wanted to post it to my brother in Canada. He loves getting things from home. A note written by our Leas Ceann Comhairle would surely raise his standing among the Irish community in Ontario. But apparently they have to keep it. I'm not really sure why. Maybe future generations of historians will want to have a look at it. As I say, I don't really know. But I didn't argue.

A Shoulder to Cry On

I NEVER know what to do when men take my hand and burst into tears.

It's always happening to me in pubs. I'm standing at the bar and the man beside me sways a little. Then he focuses on my face. "Don't tell me", he says. "Don't tell me." I never know what to tell him, so I say nothing. He sways and focuses a bit more. "Now I have ye . . . you're Your Man that does be on the telly with the little children." Already his eyes are beginning to moisten. "The little children . . . God bless them." And he looks around the pub for a Tiny Tim to lift up and brandish aloft while the little boy pipes 'God bless us each and every one.'

But there isn't a Tiny Tim in the place. There's never one around when you need one. So he takes my hand instead. I wish to God that Dublin pubs laid on an adequate supply of Tiny Tims. It would save me a whole lot of trouble. Then he starts to talk about innocence. "Their little eyes shinin' and them lookin' at you with love and trust." That's when he puts his arm around me, lays his head on my shoulder and bawls his eyes out. Sometimes I only go in for a packet of cigarettes or to use the Gents before my bus goes. I always get nabbed.

"D'ye know what I'm goin' to tell you?" That's what one man asked me. "D'ye know what I'm goin' to tell you?" It's best to say nothing because you'll never get it right. "All them little girls on your programme . . . d'ye know what they should be wearin'? Well, I'll tell ye ... communion dresses white an' pure an' innocent."

And he broke down completely. My shoulder was soaked. My shoulder is always soaked. More men soak my shoulder in Dublin pubs when I'm trying to catch my bus than any analyst could ever possibly handle.

I don't know where mothers came from. But one man suddenly brought them up. "An' every one of them little youngsters has a mammy. Cherishin' them. . . fondlin' them . . .wipin' away their little tears." And his head hit my shoulder.

"Have you got a mammy, son?"

I nodded. "Thanks be to God," he said fervently. "Everybody. . . irrespective of class or creed. . . needs a mammy." And his head hit my shoulder again.

It was in that position he sang 'A Mother's Love's A Blessing'. I joined in and speeded up the choruses. You have to move things along a bit when you've got a bus to catch.

"Atishoo! My Grandfather Caught A Cold From James Joyce in 1895"

Maybe the man is a chancer. I'm not really sure. But he's making a fortune out of overseas visitors to Dublin. He calls himself *James Joyce Coughs and Colds Ltd.* and the service he offers is absolutely unique.

The man positions himself beside foreign tourists in a Dublin pub. Then he coughs and sneezes and buys the nearest tourist a pint.

"D'ye know what I'm goin' to tell you?" he says in a conspiratorial whisper. "This cold I have on me . . . my grandfather caught this very same cold off James Joyce in 1895." He explains that his grandfather was putting in new plumbing in the Hotel Corneille over in Paris. He was ripping up the floorboards in Room 12 and this man was hunched over a typewriter in the corner. Coughing and spluttering and singing snatches of "The Rocky Road to Dublin".

"My grandfather joined in the choruses and beat time with his hammer on the waterpipes." The two men spent the night playing 25's and in the morning the man had rooked the grandfather. And the grandfather had caught his cold.

"Hang onto that cold." the man told him. "Some day it will be worth a fortune."

At this stage the overseas tourists usually finish the story in a reverend half-whisper.

"This man who gave your grandfather the cold ... this man ... he is ... James Joyce?"

"The very one," agrees your man. "And this ... this most literary of colds has been in the family ever since ."
He explains that his coughs and sneezes are now designated as National Treasures. When the mother had it she was studied by American professors. They recorded her coughing first thing in the morning on Bloomsday and used the tapes on university lecture tours. Furthermore tapes and cassettes of his own Joycean sneezes are kept under lock and key at the Smithsonian Institute.
"And nothing," he says, "nothing would give me greater pleasure than to let each one of you record a Guaranteed Irish Joycean cough." Ciné-cameras whirr, cassette recorders pick up his every splutter. And they all agree that £5 a head is nothing for capturing a National Treasure on tape.
As a bonus he shows them his cigarette. "You may have noticed," he says, "You may have noticed that I'm a chain smoker. The reason for this is simple. James Joyce gave the grandfather a light during that game of 25's in 1895 'Never let that light go out,' he said, 'someday it'll be worth a fortune.' The family has kept a cigarette on the go ever since. The same class of thing as an Olympic flame. It never goes out."
The overseas tourists agree that £2.50 a head to light off your man's cigarette is a cultural bargain.
This kind of concept is still in its infancy. If we harness W. B. Yeats properly we could pay off the National Debt.

When The Cinema Courting Had To Stop

I'd completely forgotten that people did it in the cinema. It was years since I'd been to the pictures. Everything was grand for the first thirty minutes or so. Peter O'Toole was jigging across the desert on an unnamed camel. I was sitting in the darkness marvelling at how Peter and myself had kept our looks from the sixties. The couple beside me were snuggled cosily into each other. We were all ready for a long night in Arabia with popcorn and crisps.

"Marty, don't".

I got the fright of my life. An urgent whisper from my left made me sit bolt upright. Marty was clearly losing interest in the desert and getting some experimental ideas of his own. Good girl yourself, I thought. Put in the boot while there's still time. Let him know that you'll tell your mammy. It's the only way.

I tried to keep my eyes on the screen. Omar Sharif was shooting a Bedouin for using the wrong water-hole. Marty was performing a very subtle manouevre which involved sliding both arms into position without appearing to move an inch. His girlfriend whispered another "Marty don't", but it didn't carry half as much conviction as her first one.

"I'm just getting-comfortable, Karen," he explained. He didn't look very comfortable to me. There was more of him in Karen's seat than in his own, but in the best tradition of all good snooker players he was keeping one foot on the floor.

I never know what to do in a situation like that. There are no books entitled: 'What to do when Marty and Karen declare open season in the seats beside you'. It's like having a conversation with a man who is wearing a very obvious hairpiece. The harder you try not to look, the more your eyes take on a life of their own.

Part of me wanted to say, "Easy there son — put that foot back on the floor or I'll call the manager." Another part of me was admitting to the very real danger of Marty asking does your mother stitch and calling me friend. When somebody addresses you as *pal* or *friend* in Dublin it's time to run for your life.

He was making the same kind of noises that I make when my inhaler doesn't work anymore and I'm careering headlong into bronchospasm. His right leg was invading my space on a rhythmic thirty second basis. The suicidal part of me was urging: "the next time it comes within range, grab hold of it and give it a bloody good bite".

The interval saved me. Up came the lights and Karen said it wasn't great so far. Marty assured her that the second half is only magic.

That's what I was afraid of.

Briefing The Catminder

I never realised how deep and complex the bond is between me and my three cats until I had to go away to London for a weekend. A friend of mine offered to stay in my house and as far as she was concerned, the job of cat-minding was as simple as knowing how to use a tin-opener. To be quite honest I thought it was as simple as that too until I began to explain the feline power structure to her.

Willow will only eat his food on top of the fridge. Don't ask me why because I haven't got the faintest idea. That's just the way that it is. Oh, and he won't eat anything at all unless you convince him first that his food is absolutely delicious. Put his dish on top of the fridge and say things out loud like — 'My goodness, what a truly scrumptious dinner ...I wish that I was getting that...mmmmmmmm. . . tuna . . .utterly delicious!' That should be sufficient to get him started but if he stops eating at any stage if he pauses in mid-meal you'll have to say it again with greater conviction. What we're actually describing here is talking him through his meal.

Give Hoot his food first, otherwise he will eat everyone else's. In fact give him his food in the spare bedroom if you can manage it and lock him in until Blackie and Willow have both finished theirs.

Blackie's feeding habits are much simpler. Basically speaking she will eat anything. You don't need to praise or coax or activate her. Just put down the dish and she will do the rest.

Oh — Blackie may need counselling if she comes to the front door with a mouse or something like that. You see, whenever she catches anything she is stricken with the most dreadful remorse. You will know when this happens because you will hear a muffled meow full of guilt and anguish on the other side of the front door. What-

ever you do, don't open it or she will be in past you like a flash with whatever it is that she has captured.
Please talk to her through the letter box and reassure her that it's not her fault. She needs to hear things like: "Try not to upset yourself Blackie, it's your nature and you're more or less stuck with it. That's what cats do. We still love you. No, I'm not just saying that...I really mean it."
My friend was looking at me in a way that she has never looked before. And I still hadn't told her about Willow, the Four Horsemen of the Apocalypse and the front door bell.
Please leave the sitting room door and the hot press open at all times because that is Willow's escape route if anybody rings the front doorbell. Once again I don't know why but he seems to believe that somebody or something is coming to get him, it may be The Four Horsemen, it may be the Hounds of the Baskerville's, he never really said, but that's the way that it is. Oh — and if you' re watching television, the same rules apply because if anybody rings a doorbell in a TV programme he takes to the hot press as well.
It is quite amazing how much you learn about yourself when you are leaving week-end instructions behind you. And I still hadn't covered squatter's rights.
Far be it from me to tell you where you should or shouldn't sit...I mean you are being good enough to hold the fort for me while I'm away...nonetheless, the beanbag belongs to Willow, the rocking-chair to Blackie and Hoot lies upside down on the third step of the stairs with his legs thrust up in the air so do be careful not to

break your neck when you're coming downstairs in the morning. I think that's about it...oh...just in case I didn't mention it already, if a grey cat comes to the door do not let him in. He thinks that he lives here but the others know that he doesn't and you'll need the firebrigade to get the four of them apart. Do have a nice weekend and I'll see you on Monday.

Crash Helmets For Spiders

God-fearing folk are up in arms. Saying it shouldn't be allowed. Calling for the deportation or incarceration or worse of Micilin Mac an Bhosca. He is quite unconcerned about the whole business. "That's progress," he said. "Ireland giving the lead to the rest of the world. Where's the harm in that?" His objectors don't agree. "It's pagan," they replied. "Pagan, pure and simple."
Nobody really minded when Micilin sprayed flies with a very fine aerosol. It didn't do them any harm. A fine spray of liquidised latex and essence of elastic. The flies still walked upside-down across ceilings and did all the things that flies love to do. Not a bother on them.
Micilin Mac an Bhosca was content to wait for nature to take its course. He had filled his house with spiders and the aerosol-sprayed flies. He knew that he was on to something when a spider spun its way down from the ceiling on a single strand then suddenly whammed back up again. It walloped its head against the roof but didn't say anything because that is not in the nature of the insect. But its eyes glazed over. It was concussed and that bothered Mac an Bhosca on two levels: compassionate

and productive. Nobody would wish concussion on a spider. A concussed spider does not spin elastic. Micilin's joy was qualified.

His house was filled with spiders twanging up and down from the roof. Spinning miles and miles of high-grade elastic. But at any one time, three out of every ten spiders were unconscious. And that's what got the objectors going.

"Upsetting the balance of nature," they said. "Almighty God never intended spiders to brain themselves against ceilings."

Mac an Bhosca conceded on that point And he manufactured very ingenious miniature crash helmets. Scaled down from the real thing. Padded with sponge and strapped very gently onto his spiders.

There now followed a tiny thud when they whammed against the roof but this time their eyes remained bright and alert. They didn't glaze over. Micilin had answered his critics. But they still weren't happy.

"This is making a mockery out of the insect world. Next thing he'll be putting leather jackets and rocker boots onto them. Where will it all end?" they asked. And well they might.

Mac an Bhosca is now experimenting with pasta. Trying to convert it into an aerosol spray. Thinking ahead to a very slender spaghetti for people on a diet. "Spiders will prefer spinning spaghetti," says Micilin. "Cos they won't need crash helmets." The man could well be right.

This is far worse than Peeping Toms

Denzil Hahesy was sitting in the bath. Vigorously scrubbing his back with a loofa.

Suddenly he felt very, very uneasy. Almost as if he was being watched. He swung around just in time to see three or four little heads ducking out of sight at the window.

Rachel Hahesy was getting ready for bed. Suddenly she felt it too. "Denzil," she hissed. "Put that book down and protect my honour!"

He grabbed a hurling stick and crept down into the back garden. Over the hedge he could see a neighbour in striped pyjamas clutching a cricket bat. He was protecting his wife's honour as well.

But they didn't find anyone. The gardens were deserted apart from a robin, two pigeons and a sparrow.

A line of cars was parked on Dollymount Strand. Two o'clock in the morning. Springs creaking. Windows steamed up. Occupants saying things like: " Oh Kevin." "Oh Brigid." "Oh Marty."

Suddenly one car was silent. A girl whispered: "Shamey, there's someone out there watching us. Find your socks and protect my honour."

He eased the door open, crawled out and wriggled on his stomach around to the back of the car. Men were doing the same all along the beach, ready to pounce on whoever or whatever was there. But the beach was deserted apart from six gulls, two curlews and a Brent Goose.

Gradually, almost imperceptibly, people became very jumpy. Suddenly swinging around in the bus queue and snarling at complete strangers: "What are you lookin' at?" Back would come the reply: "I'm lookin' at you, your eyes are blue, your face is like a kangaroo!"
Things were far from good.
It was Denzil Hahesy who began to fit the pieces together. He was planting seed cabbages in the garden when he noticed a sparrow peeping in through an upstairs window. The sparrow twittered once or twice and another one landed beside it. Then another. And another. They formed a little queue hopping up and down in their eagerness to get a good look inside. They appeared to be tweeting remarks to each other and falling around the windowsill.
Then he noticed a pair of robins next door. They were standing on each others shoulders to have a peep into the kitchen. Further down the road a couple of raggy crows were peering into a bathroom and nudging one another.
Denzil is no fool. He knew he was witnessing a scaled-down version of what is happening all over Ireland. The birds are striking back. They've had enough of humans with binoculars hiding in bushes. Spying on them as they snuggle up in their nests. Using microphones to record their intimate little loving tweets.
We have brought this on ourselves. You can push a sparrow so far.

We Can Do Without Scoundrels Like This

A lot of people saw it happen. And they backed up the bus conductor's story. Otherwise he would have been heavily sedated and asked to lie on a couch and talk about early adolescent encounters in hay stacks. The bus was coming down Grafton Street. An old woman wearing a fox-stole was sitting alone. The man behind her was feeling very uneasy. "The way the bloody fox kept staring at me," he said. "No matter which way I looked, its eyes seemed to be following mine."

He repeated quietly to himself: "Fox-stoles are deceased — there is nothing to worry about". That was when the stole completely wrecked his composure. "The shaggin' thing winked at me."

He later swore this on his mother's grave: "May God strike me down if I tell a lie". That was when he asked the old woman on the bus if he could see the fox-stole's death certificate. The stole bit a lump out of the conductor's leg but not before he yelled down to the driver: "Open the doors, Kevin, and let it out!"

The fox hurtled off up Grafton Street with the old woman giving chase. She was protesting loudly: "I've been done — me fox-stole isn't decently dead!"

A watching garda wrote something significant in his notebook and said nothing.

The same garda was queuing with his tray in a self-service restaurant two days later, off-duty. When the old woman in front of him reached the checkout a row developed.

"That fox around your neck ate three ham rolls and a chocolate eclair." The check-out girl was adamant: "I seen it with me own two eyes."
...The old woman said: "Don't be so ridiculous — I've only just bought it and foxstoles can't eat anything because they're dead". The fox chose that moment to make a fierce liar out of her by grabbing a meringue and legging it out onto the street. The garda wrote something in his notebook. The old women were different. So were the fox-stoles. But each fox had a lump on its head. Somebody was clearly up to something.
The furrier in Camden Street confessed to everything. He was whacking foxes over the head with a hockey stick. Then he was selling them as very expensive foxstoles. When the foxes recovered consciousness it was usually night time and their new owners were asleep. So they headed back to the shop and crept in through a cat door. Each fox had a keenly developed homing instinct and a splitting headache. The furrier had sold one fox six times in the same week. The foxes had Sundays off.
Some old women are now bringing a stethoscope with them when they buy a stole. You can't really blame them.

The Return Of The Wild Geese

They were wild when they got here. But I have my doubts about them now. Plump Brent Geese all the way from Greenland and Arctic Canada. God alone knows why they picked Dublin 3 for their winter break, but that's the way it is. Wild untamed geese flying through blizzards and storms at sea with one thought in their minds . . . we've got to make it to Clontarf. And I don't think they'll ever go home again. The crack here is too good.

They huddle in little groups along the grass ribbon at Dollymount seafront and watch the joggers wobbling past. They don't have sights like that in Arctic Canada. The Brent geese just love overweight wobblers in tracksuits. They make little chortling goose noises and nudge one another. Some of them topple onto their backs and lie on the grass with their legs twitching in the air. Tears stream down their feathery cheeks.

Lots of Brent geese are DART fanatics. They line the railway embankment at Fairview and wave their wings at the driver. When he toots the horn they're utterly thrilled. Some of them regularly try to sneak on board the DART at Killester Station but the porter hunts them with a sweeping brush and shouts "Shoo!" They only do it to get a good chase.

They do worse than that. It gets very boring in Clontarf when the DART has stopped running and the joggers have all gone home, so after midnight they ring doorbells with their beaks and scuttle down to the front gate. When the door opens they make derisive goose noises and stick out their tongues Some of them prefer to perch on upstairs windows sills and peer in at people going to bed. They know the best windows by now.

Naturalists and ornithologists are worried. These birds appear to be defying the law of nature which says they return home to Greenland. None of them want to fly any further than Booterstown DART station. They stand on the platform for hours admiring themselves on the special bird-watchers' display board. It is time for the people of Clontarf to start shouting: "Shoo," at the top of their voices before the balance of nature is destroyed entirely.

Puffing Bunnies

The temptation is to use words like 'sensational' and 'amazing'. But professor Jethraim Karbeovah is not like that. For six years now he has been quietly researching the effects of cigarette smoking on women. Using rabbits.

Ten female rabbits, were removed from their mothers as soon as they were old enough. Each of them was then kept in the strictest isolation. No contact whatsoever with other rabbits. "In this way, none of them has ever had any sex," says the professor. "Each of the rabbits is a virgin bunny!"

The ten rabbits were trained to puff cigarette smoke from a rubber tube, inhale deeply and blow it out again. They each smoked the equivalent of 20 cigarettes a day. " Aha!" say the purists. "This wasn't a valid test because the virgin bunnies didn't smoke real cigarettes." The professor points quite reasonably to the danger of the rabbits setting fire to their straw and incinerating themselves before the experiment had run its course.

The professor carefully monitored the rabbits' progress. On July 27 1981, he made this amazing discovery. "At first one, then three and finally four of the rabbits had become pregnant . . each of them was expecting little bunnies." The professor did not rush into print with the announcement: 'Cigarette Smoking Can Make You Pregnant'. He didn't wish to jump to any hasty conclusions. Instead he examined the rabbits' food intake. Each of them had been fed an exclusive diet of cabbage, carrots and dandelion leaves. Which led to this cautious statement from the professor: "If you eat nothing else but cabbage, carrots and dandelion leaves while smoking 20 or more cigarettes a day, there exists a real possibility that it will make you pregnant."

The professor doesn't wish to cause an ureasoning panic. "The chances of unwanted pregnancies are slight," he says. "Because very few women munch carrots, cabbage, dandelion leaves and nothing else."

But he claims that this method of conception can be a great boon for women whose husbands are away climbing mountains or working on oil rigs. Already, all sorts of legal questions have arisen. If a pregnancy occurs as a result of a woman using the Karbeovah Carrot, Cabbage and Dandelion Leaf Method, who is the father? Supposing an unwanted pregnancy occurs . . . can the mother initiate a paternity suit against the major tobacco companies? Somebody will have to answer these questions. There is a lot more to this than meets the eye.

Why Irish Cows Have Failed The Nation

HIS NEIGHBOURS didn't know what he was at. They watched Reginald Thwisk mixing coffee beans and grass seed. Then he ploughed up The Long Meadow and the Lady Acre. They peered over the hedge as Thwisk sowed his coffee bean and grass seed mixture. Far into the night he watered the Lady Acre with liquidised sugar. Then he hung a sign on the gate: 'White with Sugar.'

And he turned half his dairy herd loose into the field. "Ye can be my white coffee with sugar cows," he said. And he tagged their ears so that he'd know which cows were which. The rest of the herd went into to the Long Meadow which didn't get a drop of liquid sugar. They were his 'white coffee-without' cattle.

Thwisk invited representatives from all the leading hotels and restaurants to attend his milking shed on the great day. They queued up with their plastic cups as he milked Ermintrude — a white coffee with sugar cow. One by one they announced their verdict. The coffee was indeed instant but it was luke warm. Thwisk had to admit that their verdict was a true one.

He experimented further by stampeding his cows up and down the fields until their tails swished and steam billowed from their nostrils. Then he milked them immediately. Ermintrude and Martha and Penelope gave piping hot coffee. But as he worked his way through the herd, the cows began to cool down and so did the coffee.

Thwisk was now hot on the trail. He built a huge treadmill in the milkshed. It worked on the waterwheel principle and was large enough to take one cow at a time. The theory was simple. You installed your cow and shoute: "Hup Hup … g'wan outta that!" Then you played a 'Hup-Hupping' tape while the cow went like a whirlwind on the treadmill. As soon as her nostrils steamed you slammed on the brakes and milked her into a vacuum flask which kept the coffee on the boil.
Aer Lingus were very impressed with the idea of in-flight cows on each plane. Truly instant coffee. The treadmill could even generate emergency power in the event of engine failure.
Hoteliers had preliminary talks with Thwisk about installing instant coffee cows in their kitchens. And that was when it happened. One of the caterers asked the crucial question: "What about black coffee Mr. Thwisk?" And the great man groaned. He was forced to admit: "There be no such thing as a black coffee cow — with or without."
Thwisk is now feeding paperclips to his pigs. God alone knows what he's at.

This Couple Can Make Ireland Great

It was single-decker buses mostly. Large trucks and vans as well. Causing hold-ups on narrow country roads. Cars couldn't get past them and minor convoys formed. Which was how Kevin Hahesy thought of it.
"By the Lord Harry," he said, "if I can't go round the bus, why can't I go over it?" And he drew diagrams.

Pictures of single-decker buses with a ramp up the front and a ramp down the back. He suggested that you can only overtake vehicles across the top if they're heading in the same direction as yourself. "Otherwise you'd have cars crashing into each other on the roofs of buses and then where would we be?"

Bus Eireann shot Kevin's idea down in flames. "Have a bit of sense," they said. "Do you think we're running a stunt circus or what?" Kevin told them they had a unique chance to be in the vanguard of a dynamic new notion in traffic flow. "This could well be the Year of The Ramp," he said.

"That's as maybe," they said. "But what about motorists who drive up onto the roof of a bus and stay there to save a bit of petrol?"

Kevin was snookered. He couldn't think of anything so he asked his wife. "I have it," she said. "Build bridges at certain points along each route with just enough clearance for a singledecker bus to pass under. That'd get them down in a hurry. All other traffic would be free to use slip roads around the bridges but the buses would be obliged to go under them."

Kevin embraced her and drew some more diagrams. Pictures of bridges ... buses approaching them with cars on top. Bus Eireann said you can't go round doing things like that even if a car refuses to come down off the roof of your bus. You can't go through life whacking them against bridges. And there the whole thing might have ended. But Kevin Hahesy had a dream. So had his wife. Both of them believed in the Year of the Ramp. They fitted one to the front and one to the back of their

van. Next day Mrs. Hahesy sped along the Dingle to Tralee road.
Kevin followed close behind on his motor bike.
"OK Brigid," he shouted. "I'm coming over the top."
"Give it the gun Kevin," she yelled and he opened the throttle. What followed was sheer poetry, providing you weren't directly involved in it.
Kevin Hahesy's flight was as brief as it was beautiful. He has never fully understood how he cleared the van without actually touching the roof. He doesn't know how he arrived in Dingle inside a travelling bank while his wife reached Tralee in their van with his motorbike on the top.
"Be God Brig," he said. "I think we're onto something if we can sort out what exactly happened." If he draws some diagrams it might help.

Are You On It?

I got this fierce urge to play a game of 'Tip and Tig'. Grafton Street was packed. I tipped a complete stranger and said: "You're on it!" His eyes lit up and people scattered in all directions. A lot of them made for Stephen's Green and hid in the bushes. A newspaper seller charged into Switzers and locked himself in the toilet.
The man I tipped got a bus down to O'Connell Street where nobody knew about it yet. He touched a woman's shoulder and yelled: "You're on it!" and the mad scatter happened all over again. People poured out of Clerys as she rushed the front entrance. "Will someone for God's

sake let me tip them?" she yelled. "I have to go home and get the husband's dinner."

A garda went in to investigate the sudden rush through the exits. Even the shop assistants had abandoned their posts. The woman stood there crying.

The Garda approached her, talking quietly. Like lightening she tipped him. It was a trap. The garda radioed headquarters. "I'm on it, lads,'' he said.

The effect of 'Tip and Tig' on the city centre was like a bomb scare. Some people got taxis home but only after they had proved to the driver that they weren't on it. Nobody was taking any chances. People peeped anxiously around corners and asked: "Who's on it?" Rumours spread like wildfire.

One dentist didn't have a solitary patient all day because somebody said it was him. There was uproar on the Cork train and many people abandoned it at Limerick Junction. But all in all it was much too ragged. National 'Tip and Tig' must be better organised.

The game will start from Áras an Uachtaráin. The President shall deliver the first ceremonial tip and declare: "You're on it," in Irish. The person who is tipped shall wear the official 'Tip and Tig' bleeper so that the security forces can monitor him at all times. We don't want him leaving the country. A tip in the wrong place could cause an international incident.

National 'Tip and Tig' shall bring us closer together. Every night before closedown, RTE will announce who's on it and show his or her photograph. Certain places will be out of bounds. Running into a hospital

and tipping a patient will be forbidden; especially if the patient's on traction.
Tourists will be obliged to wear special badges and must not be tipped. An unguarded moment, a careless tip and before we know where we are, our national 'Tip and Tig' could be swiped by a foreign power. If they want to play it let them go and organise a game of their own.
If you shout *Pax* and cross your fingers you shall enjoy complete immunity. But only if you're having a baby or transplanting a set of kidneys.
This country has got far too many hurlers on the ditch as it is.

Weight Watch

A lot of people are doing it. Losing weight and saying: "Thanks be to God it's gone". As far as they're concerned, that's the end of it. But it's not. And the sooner we accept this fact the better.
When we exercise vigorously we perspire, and the weight which we shed vaporises and enters the atmosphere. "It forms a very fine invisible cloud," said Rufus Madigan, "which is waiting for one thing ... the chance to make a comeback." Rufus is the author of a highly controversial book *Other People's Lost Weight Is Trying To Get You.* He maintains that everytime we remove our clothing we are at risk.
"Weight vapour can't penetrate people's clothes and the only chance it has of reattaching itself is when we bare our limbs." Rufus recommends that we prance and leap

around the bedroom while undressing. If you stand still you're asking for trouble.
He has estimated that as a nation we lose many thousands of tons of weight every year through regular exercises. "This in turn is transformed into vapour which wanders around the place until it finds suitable recipients. Which explains why so many young babies are chubby and bouncing. They're so often uncovered that they have little or no protection. The weight which a jogger lost in Bandon yesterday could well make a fighting comeback in Holles St. Hospital tomorrow."
Football matches and beauty contests are favourite hunting grounds for lost weight vapour. Rufus had detected huge concentrations of it at Lansdowne Road at the precise moment that the players remove their track suits. "Footballers are very aware of the danger," he explains. "This is why they jig up and down so much while being introduced to dignitaries."
Weight vapour is present in huge quantities at the Miss World contest. It surrounds the ramp in a dense cloud and waits for the girls to appear in their swimsuits. "And this," says Rufus, "this is where the ingenuity of the vapour proves itself. It only attaches a couple of milligrams to each girl so that she couldn't possibly detect a weight gain afterwards."
There is only one recorded instance to date of weight vapour becoming over-excited and behaving rashly. An insurance consultant in Dingle was relaxing so totally in the bath that he fell asleep. When he woke an hour later, most of the water had overflowed. A small but very powerful crane was required to raise him to his feet and

the bathroom door had to be widened with a sledge hammer.
"This is an isolated case," says Rufus, "and need not worry us unduly." A hot shower is infinitely safer because you can jig up and down.

Upper Halves

Some shops don't have counters anymore. They prefer an open-plan with the assistants wandering around amongst the racks. This has not come a moment too soon. Many shop assistants are only used to dealing with the top halves of people. They only ever see us from the waist up. For this reason a lot of them have developed an unreasoning fear of people's bottom halves. They even say it in their morning prayers. "God bless Daddy and Mammy and keep me safe this day from the menace of other persons from the waist down."
They feel safe and secure in behind their counters. Some of them bring flasks of tea and banana sandwiches so they can stay in there at lunchtime. Last year in a Dublin shoeshop my mother absentmindedly wandered in behind the counter. The shop assistant shot up a ladder three steps at a time and crouched on the top step. He shouted: "Out damn spot," and pelted my mother with ballet shoes. This has had a profound and a lasting effect on her. She now goes to Mass barefoot with her boots slung around her neck.
"My terror of people's bottom-halves nearly wrecked my marriage," one girl confessed. "As far as I was

concerned I had only married my husband from the waist up. I even had a counter built in the kitchen. We only ever communicated with each other when he was on one side and I was on the other."
Her husband realised that something was gravely wrong with their relationship when she introduced the cardboard box. He was obliged to walk round the house inside it.
"The box came up to my waist," he recalled. "with two holes cut out for my feet." The marriage counsellor observed that cardboard boxes play no part whatsoever in the great divine marital plan. "How can a husband even hope to put out the bin in that yoke?" he asked.
Bank cashiers who sit on high stools suffer from the same problem in reverse. Most of their bottom half is out of sight and tucked away under the counter.
They have subconsciously disowned themselves from the waist down. '"They feel accepted by members of the public from the waist up," says an industrial psychologist "but live in terror that people will reject the rest of them." This is why so many bank cashiers stand behind low walls and hedges when talking to the opposite sex
"My boyfriend would only ever meet me in a field in Connemara or in the deep end of a swimming pool," one girl complained bitterly.
"On the day we got married he hid behind the wall outside the church for the wedding pictures." She doesn't know what she's going to tell the children.
"Why is daddy always standing behind low walls and hedges?"

"Because he works in a bank." Is it any wonder our children are confused?

If You Need New Tyres...

"The best time for it is between half past four and six o'clock in the morning," he told me. "I always do it around that time," he said. "It's lovely and quiet and there's hardly anyone around."
I hadn't a clue what he was talking about and a wrong guess would leave you further up the creek than any man has ever gone before. He explained that he takes his car out of the garage on the dot of four thirty every morning. Then he drives it very slowly up the road on the wrong side for a precise measured distance. His wife walks in front with a red lamp in her hand. "To make absolutely certain there's no danger to anybody coming from the opposite direction." As soon as he reaches a predetermined stopping point, he turns the car and heads for home — still driving on the wrong side of the road. "Herself remains a steady 50 yards in front with the lamp."
He explained that he's been picking up rubber like this for years. "Every car that uses the public highway leaves a very minute layer of rubber behind it. Thousands of cars every day. Each one shedding tiny deposits of rubber." He said you have to remember that the cars on each side of the road are travelling in the same direction. So the rubber is laid down with a uniform thread. "All you need to do is drive against the thread and you can pick up as much rubber as you need."

You learn by your mistakes. He said he took his brand new car out the very first night he bought it. And every night after that. And he drove for miles and miles on the wrong side of the road. His eldest son cycled slowly in front with the red lamp. "I didn't realise that the bloody tyres were growing until they started to jam against the mudguards."
That was when he worked it out. You keep an exact record of your frontwards mileage during the day. Then you cover the exact same distance on the other side of the road in the wee small hours when everybody is asleep except you and your wife and the eldest son.
In a democratic marriage you can take turns out front with the lamp. "Once you get your sums right," he said, "the same set of tyres will do you forever."
CIE nearly hit on the secret when the traffic flow was reversed along the city quays. The buses that go up and down to Heuston Station all day were suddenly going down and up instead. The tyres began to grow. But it wore off again on the way back to the garage before they hit the mudguard.
If this thing catches on nobody will get any sleep.

Read This And You'll Never Scratch Again

Some people don't believe him. But that doesn't bother Adolphus Skinner. He's far too busy checking out the infrastructure inside a Tremble.

"That's the collective term we use," he explained. "A colony of itches is called a Tremble."
Adolphus now wishes to learn how exactly the itches spend their day inside it. "Beavers build dams; bees make honey; but what do itches get up to in their colonies?" It's as if he can peer in and make notes.
After first establishing that an itch is a form of energy, he then found they have origins high up in the Stratosphere.
"That's where they group together into vast energy fields," Aolphus told his uncle Kevin. "And these groupings are your Trembles." Uncle Kevin said: "Would you for God's sake get yourself a proper job and stop all this demented talk before you have us all worn out with the scratching".
But Adolphus was on the verge of his great breakthrough. "Oxygen!" he shrieked. "That's it! That's what they do all day." And he drew a diagram of them inhaling huge quantities of it from the atmosphere.
"Then they expand to contain it and never ever release it again."
This is why mountain climbers become breathless and athletes are gasping after a race. He also hints at a possible link between Trembles of itches and asthma.
"How," he asks, "can we induce them to return all that life-giving oxygen to the atmosphere?"
He still hasn't found the answer but his itch institute at Termonfeckin is experimenting by puncturing simulated Trembles with knitting needles He still has a long way to go on this one.

Several Swedish experts agree with Adolphus on one point. Itches do not spend their whole lifetime irritating humans. 95% of it is spent up in the stratosphere swiping our oxygen.
"This leads to feelings of isolation," says Gunnar Svennsson. "They need human companionship. No itch is an island."
The tragedy is that nature only allows them one go. An itch can only let you have it once, something similar to a bee.
A terrible train of events is set in motion when it quits a tremble and gravitates downwards. The itch enters you and me and lies dormant. Sometimes for years. Then it develops a sense of well-being.
"I Belong! ... I Belong!
Suddenly the excitement surges and it overheats. Then comes the supreme act of rejection. We scratch.

Don't Bring Up Your Children This Way

She didn't realise the effect it would have. She thought it was fun. At the time it probably was. Whenever Brigid Hahesy was out walking with her youngest son, she'd say "Look, Kevin ... look at the face on the front of that lorry." And together they'd see it. The headlights were the eyes. The grille or the bumper formed the mouth. During Kevin's formative years he saw happy lorries, sad lorries, ecstatic trucks, suicidal bread-vans, insecure buses and manic milk-floats.

Brigid should have seen it coming. Especially when Kevin was very late home from school. One day when he finally arrived he was attached to a lorry-driver's thumb and fingers by the left ear.
"I found this brat" said the driver, "He was ramming gob-stoppers up the exhaust pipe of me truck." Kevin explained everything.
He was walking home when the lorry sighed and looked at him with a trembling bumper. So he tried to cheer it up with the gobstoppers. Brigid stressed that no matter how inconsolable a lorry may be, you don't go through life ramming things like that up its exhaust.
"When the lorry starts, those yokes will come hurtling out and knock somebody off their bike," she said.
The lorry driver had a cup of tea. When he went outside again he muttered at his truck before he could stop himself. "Don't you look at me like that or I'll reposition your gobstoppers." This thing was catching.
Brigid still didn't see it coming when in later years Kevin was very late home from a disco. When the phone rang the foreman at the local bus garage was in bits. "Your son is down here singing to the buses. He's trying to get the cleaners to serenade them as well."
Brigid went down the road. Lots of buses were parked outside the garage. Kevin explained that they were shivering. "They've just been washed in cold water," he said.
The foreman said: "We're trying to run a bus garage here and how the hell can we do that when people wander round outside singing to the buses and putting talcum powder on them. I can't cope with the likes of that."

When Brigid finally saw it coming it was much too late. She listened while defence counsel explained to the judge. The only reason why Kevin kept bringing lorries home was that they looked miserable. This also applied to the buses. And the morose petrol tanker. He suggested a possible solution. "Perhaps all heavy vehicle owners can in future paint happy faces on the front." You can't be too careful what you tell your children nowadays.

Suffering Ducks

It's not good enough. We must speak out boldly. Our environment is being wrecked and we are doing nothing about it. Only last week a cousin of mine was fishing for tench in the Grand Canal. "I heard this noise further upstream," he said. "And took it to be a small high powered motor boat."
The distant buzz became an insistent pulsing throb which came closer and closer. Around the corner hurtled a duck. "Its head was thrust forward and its feathers were flattened back as it zoomed into the straight." My cousin said it seemed to open up some sort of an inbuilt throttle as it accelerated and surged off upstream. He estimates that it shot underneath the bridge at upwards of 75 knots before throttling back to take the next bend. Reports have been pouring into the Department of the Environment ever since. Reports of high speed water fowl careering along the Grand Canal at breakneck speed. Some ducks float limply after colliding with lock gates. One lock-keeper explained: "You see this feath-

ered projectile powering its way towards the lock. You yell: 'Stop duck! Stop before ye concuss yourself agin me gates.' But the ducks is goin' too fast to hear ye."

Many lock-keepers have installed wooden ramps which slope up and over the lock. The duck is whizzed through the air by his own momentum to splash down safely on the other side. But this arrangement is only feasible in country areas.

The experimental ramp at Dublin's Baggot Street Bridge was dismantled because bus drivers were complaining. "We didn't mind the ducks whipping across our line of vision too much," said a spokesman. "You only ever saw a blur anyway. What we couldn't take was the tension — the white hot tension as you approached the bridge. Some ducks whacked against the side of your bus or crashed in through the windows."

They tried leaving the windows open and asking upstairs passengers to lie on the floor. But this led to problems because too many passengers wanted to lie down beside the same person.

Many Grand Canal ducks are travelling so fast that their feathers are beginning to smoulder and scorch. Wisps of blue smoke are appearing. There is an ever-present danger of ducks bursting into flames. The Department of the Environment have placed buckets of iced water on key bridges. Passers-by are asked to keep a sharp lookout for overheating ducks and douse them at the first signs of danger.

However, this is merely placing the responsibility where it does not belong. We are not to blame. The shameless dumpers of chemical waste into our canals and rivers must be fearlessly rooted out before we become the laughing stock of Europe. Tourists from overseas are not blind. They notice things. A duck with blue smoke pouring from its feathers is not a good advertisement for this country. If they spontaneously combust we'll be destroyed altogether.

Do You Moo on Holidays?

I don't know where all the people were. Seventy men, women and children live on the island. Vatersay — a tiny pinprick on the map. Up among the Hebrides. "By Jove," said the elderly Englishman with the country squire suit. Tweedy plus fours tucked into thick woolen socks. "By Jove" echoed his tweedy wife. I think they were referring to the wild grandeur of the place. We were approaching the landing stage in a small motor launch. There wasn't a soul to be seen.

"Where are all the people?" I asked the ferryman.

"They'll be all at home," he said. But I couldn't see any houses. Myself and By Jove and his wife landed and increased the island population — by three. The ferryman said he'd be back in six hours.

The elderly English couple set off at a fierce pace. Stout walking shoes. Binoculars. Soon they were lost amongst the crags and the cliffs and if there was any Spanish treasure they'd find it first.

One thing bothered me. There wasn't a single tree on the island. Any amount of cows and bulls and calves wandering free but no trees. The cattle watched my every move. God knows how many pairs of moo cow eyes followed my passage across a flat green plain. It was the bulls with the swishy tails that worried me the most. Maybe that was why the place was so deserted. It makes sound sense to stay at home when the bulls are swishing their tails and there are no trees for shinning up in a hurry.

Sitting on top of a tall sand dune. The sea on one side and an island full of cattle surrounding the other. I made an experimental friendly sort of a cow noise. A deep kind of a meaningful moo. All the cows raised their heads and listened. It was a brand new voice to them. Life probably gets boring on a tiny Hebridean Island when you know all the moos inside out. I released another one. A majestic moo that seemed to cry out for a response. And by God I got one. One by one the cows raised their heads and gave me their heartfelt best. The bulls didn't seem to mind in the least. They just bellowed and swished their tails. Maybe I was taking the pressure off them for a while. I felt all powerful on top of my sand dune. It's the ultimate buzz when you orchestrate a mixed moo-cow choir.

By Jove and his wife didn't find any treasure. They told the ferryman that the Island's cattle sounded bothered. Like they badly needed to be milked. That's not what the cows told me.

Senior Citizens May Have To Live Up Trees

My mother doesn't imagine things. When she hears noises in the night, they are definitely there. When

bedlam breaks out in the next bedroom even though there's nobody in there, I trust my mother's judgement. She knows two crows when she sees them.
When she opened the door to investigate, she saw one raggy crow perched on the dressing-table. It's partner had settled quite happily onto the bedrail. Everything knock-overable in the room had been knocked over. It was very late at night. The window was closed.
My mother is a charitable woman. She is prepared to give two crows the benefit of a reasonable doubt. Her face softened when she saw the broken ruins of their nest in the fireplace. "Ah you poor birds," she said. "You must have fallen down the chimney." The crows didn't react to this gentle understanding. They settled more easily into their perched positions. They were clearly getting dug in for the night. Opportunists. "Our nest is wrecked ... this room isn't being used for anything ... centrally heated ... your woman should be good for a bit of breakfast in the morning." My mother is a reasonable woman. "I need this room for when my son stays the night ... your feathers will only give him asthma. I don't mind you falling down my chimney ... that could happen to the best of us. I'm going to open the window now and if you're not gone by the time I count up to ten, I'm getting my walking stick." The birds didn't budge. Perhaps they are well used to senior citizens counting up to ten and brandishing walking sticks at them. I can't really be sure.
My mother rang two good friends. "I know it's very late but can you come round right away. Oh, and bring your walking sticks with you." I didn't actually witness it but

I'm certain it was an awe-inspiring sight. Three senior citizens hunting a pair of crows round and round a bedroom with their walking sticks. I'm not sure what they were shouting but I think it was "Shoo! Shoo!" The birds fled. I don't blame them.
My mother is convinced that it was an accident. She believes that the crows were rocking and rolling in their nest when it suddenly gave way. I don't. A near neighbour of hers discovered two starlings in her bedroom last week. Plus a shattered nest in the fireplace. This is too much of a coincidence. I believe that these birds are falling down senior citizens' chimneys on purpose. Looking for a bit of comfort. Central heating if they can get it. If this carry-on gets any worse it's high time that our senior citizens hit back. Let them borrow ladders and build tree houses. It's the only thing some birds understand.

What Have Landlords Got Against This Man?

Landlords keep firing him out of his flat. Soon there will be no place left for him to live. Unless Angus Cobble significantly changes his ways, he'll be out on the street. None of this would have happened but for a chance remark in a pub.
"Bees buzz." That's what the stranger said. "And they're mentioned in 'The Lake Isle of Innisfree'." The stranger

said that this was very significant. "And what about our good friend the wasp?" he continued.
"He buzzes as well," said Angus.
"Now ye have me," the stranger was very excited. "The wasp buzzes and Vaughan Williams composed 'The Wasps' Overture'." He said that this was just as significant. Creative people totally ignore non-assertive insects. Nobody writes poems about worms because a worm never stung man, woman or child. Nobody paints pictures of caterpillars because they never nip a lump out of your leg. Unless you assert yourself as an insect, the likes of W. B. Yeats and Vaughan Williams don't want know about you.
"By God, but you're right," shouted Angus. He climbed up onto a bar stool and roared: "What about our good friend the earwig?! Is there any man present who will strike a blow of liberation for the caterpillar?!" The barman told Angus he was throwing him out for his own good: "before someone hits you a dig."
It was a major turning point in Angus Cobble's life. That very night he commenced assertion training for insects in his flat. He started in a small way. Teaching spiders to thump their feet down when they walk. "Raise up your legs as high as they'll go," he told them, "and bring your feet down with a mighty stamp." Then he trained them to move across maximum noise surfaces like saucepan lids and empty biscuit tins. The spiders responded with a will.
Soon there were ninety-six of them earnestly drilling in Angus Cobble's flat. Marching vigorously in two by

twos. The floor boards creaked and trembled. Lumps of plaster fell off the ceiling in the flat below.
When Angus simultaneously trained woodworms to munch with wild abandon, the noise level was deafening. "Keep up lads!" he shouted "Assert yourselves and soon they'll be writing symphonies about you."
Some of the woodworms blunted their teeth on tubular steel chairs. The others demolished a table, Angus Cobble's walking stick and seriously weakened the floor. The next march past of ninety-six assertive spiders did the rest.
The people who lived downstairs weren't amused. "That class of a thing is agin nature," they said. "Bloody spiders and termites and lumps of rubble everywhere." Angus Cobble is looking for a basement flat. He may never train insects again.

It Shouldn't Happen To A Hare

He couldn't believe his eyes. A man I know was crouching down behind a sandhill on Bull Island . . . right in the very heart of the bird sanctuary. Lovingly he lined up a Greater Crested Whelk Warbler in his camera sights. He was just about to photograph this almost extinct species when a hare hopped across his line of vision. Up to its knees in seawater.
"The bloody thing came splashing along like some thing out of a David Bowie video and put the heart across my lovely Whelk Warbler," said the bird watcher. This is not an isolated incident. The ornithologists of

Bull Island are up in arms. " It's getting so you just can't take a decent picture of a seabird anymore because the hares keep screwing things up," said a man who lost a priceless shot of a North Carolina Noodle Crake when a hare cartwheeled across the feeding grounds and balanced on his front legs.

It was even worse on Dollymount Beach last summer. "My family album is full of bleedin' hares," complained a mammy with a box camera. "Look! There's a picture of Darren and a hare, that one is Natalie and a hare, and see here, that's daddy asleep on a rug festooned with the little beggars. I've even got one of Auntie Mavis floating on her back and they're doin' the breast stroke all around her."

None of this was going on while the Carroll's Golf Tournament was being held at Royal Dublin. The media circus descended on Dollymount with lights and cameras and microphones. The hares never had it so good. "This is Gabriel Quirke, ITN News at Ten, Dollymount. Surrounded by hares." They were front paged by all the national dailies. They streaked along packed fairways while the crowds whooped and cheered. Liam Nolan mentioned them in his commentaries. The more experienced ones waited until Sevy Ballesteros was lining up a crucial nailbiting putt before hopping onto the green.

They even looked into the right television camera without anybody telling them. Then they snuggled into their burrows during the winter season and lived on their magnificent memories.

Suddenly, cruelly, it was all over. The golf tournament folded its tents and moved on to Portmarnock. Some of the hares didn't come out again for months. They withdrew into themselves. Others sat in solitary isolation in the middle of the fairways, ears drooping, shoulders hunched, until one fateful day a birdwatcher with a camera slung over his shoulder took a shortcut across the golf course. "I had to run for me life," he said. "They came at me from all sides. Millions of hares all making shapes and posing and shoving one another out of the way." Some of them are even attempting to fly since the Brent Geese arrived from Greenland. These hares can sense a front page picture a mile off.

God Help Them

I saw a little white dog with a ponytail in the middle of his forehead. A woman beside me in the bus queue was holding him in his arms. The dog's hair was gathered together so that it stood up quite straight. It looked like a tiny white fountain or a miniature unicorn's pointy bit. It was lovely.
"Excuse me," I asked. "Why has your dog got a ponytail in the front?"
"It's to keep the hair out of his eyes," the woman explained. "Otherwise he goes around the place bumping into things. He bangs his head against chairs and tables and stuns himself and then he doesn't know where he is."
I couldn't help wondering why Almighty God would create a little dog who can't see where he is going, It

didn't seem very fair to me. No dog in his right mind enjoys walking into brick walls or sideboards. "He's a tunnelling breed," she said. "The hair is meant to protect his eyes when digging."

That's all very well. But what about when he's not trying to reach the centre of the earth? What about when he wants to chase a cat up an apple tree or peer into a butcher's shop? If I ever get to heaven I'm going to ask God about it.

I'm also going to ask Him why he fitted an earwig's pincers onto the back. If the earwig wants to attack a beetle or an ant or something he has to go into reverse and then he can't see where he is going either. It certainly is not my place to tell God about earwig design but I think the least he could do is equip them with a tiny rear-view mirror.

I was watching a programme on the television about penguins last week. I think they were emperor penguins. When the mother lays her egg she gives it to the father to mind and then sets off on a weary 200 mile march to the sea in search of food. The poor father has to stand there keeping the egg warm for over two months. Himself and 50,000 other fathers all huddle together thinking: "My goodness — I hope she hurries up. That icy wind would skin you." The only sounds are ravenous rumbling stomachs and raging blizzards.

Two months later the unfortunate mother who is stuffed to exploding point with fish has to tramp the 200 miles back to feed the newly hatched baby. Then comes the part which I think is the absolute pits. The poor father doesn't get as much as a left-over sardine or

a thank you or anything. Off he goes on an empty stomach across 200 miles of polar ice to get a bit of food for himself and if I was him I wouldn't bother coming back.
Lord — thou art hard on penguins. And earwigs. And dogs with hair over their eyes.

This Is Better Than Experimenting With Animals

Nobody knows how they do it. But nothing is surer. Trees really do communicate with one another. Some scientists are very excited about it. But staff at the Royal Academy of Gort couldn't care less. "We have better things to be doing with our time," said an t-Ollamh Fergus Lint. And he released the Academy's findings on match boxes.
"The tension inside a matchbox," he announced, "Is in direct proportion to the number of matches removed. The matches feel a certain safety in numbers at the outset, but as each successive match is removed, the survivors alternate between acute tension and complete despair. The last match out is usually in bits."
"What sort of a headcase is he?" asked critics of an t-Ollamh, Fergus Lint.
"A man who says the likes of that couldn't possibly be the full shilling."
But Lint silenced them once and for all. He held an open day at the Royal Academy in Gort and revealed his Molecular Monitor to the public for the very first time.

"I am now going to attach the monitor to this dining room chair," he said. "Then I will sit on it." As he moved towards the chair an amazing thing happened. The read-out from the monitor clearly showed that the molecules in the chair were tensing themselves. And every single one, of them in the chair legs braced itself to take the strain as he sat down.

The watchers broke into spontaneous applause and one of them spoke to an t-Ollamh "Verily thou art the full shilling," he said.

Lint and his team of researchers have monitored an immense variety of things.

"Teabags" he said. "Teabags experience the same kind of tension as matches. We were quite prepared for this. But we were astonished to find that they emit short sharp bursts of coffee aroma at the precise moment that the box is opened. It's a subliminal attempt to change the person's mind about having a cup of tea.

"Teabags will try anything to survive."

Nothing was known about the complex, psychological makeup of the biro. But Lint's Molecular Monitor has revealed that no pen willingly parts with its ink. "It realises," said Lint, "that we will dump it as soon as it goes dry."

"This is the reason why nine out of ten new biros tested in a shop didn't write first time. They were holding back. An internal struggle was going on — the biro's need for fulfillment against its powerful instinct for survival."

An t-Ollamh Fergus Lint is tight-lipped about future research. "Gigot chops the moment of consumption" That's all he was prepared to say. Maybe it's enough.

About That Sound Under Your Roof

You wouldn't worry too much about moles doing it. They know exactly what they're at. Moles could honeycomb the country with tunnels and you wouldn't lose any sleep over it.

What does worry me is the existence of a top-secret file in Dublin Castle marked "Missing Persons — Believed to be Somewhere Underground." It contains a list of people known to have bought shovels and dropped out of circulation in the recent past. At present they are below ground-level digging tunnels into banks.

This is no idle fantasy. From time to time there are positive sightings. Six men suddenly appeared up through the floor of the Pro-Cathedral last Saturday morning.

"Peace to all here present," they said.

"And also with you," said the congregation.

They told the priest that they were checking the soil for Mesozoic artifacts.

"God bless the work and more power to your shovels," he said.,

"Amen," added the congregation.

Sources in Dublin Castle believe these may be the same men who materialise through the floorboards of the Round Room in the Mansion House during a meeting of The Irish Asthma Society.

"Eastern Health Board", they said. "Routine check for cat and feathers." These men are very convincing. They even borrowed a cylinder of pure oxygen before reversing at speed back down the tunnel.
The problem of detecting these people is immense. At first, the authorities were content to wait for cave-ins. The kind of thing that happened during the St. Patrick's Day parade at Tinahely last year. The entire St. Stanislaus Fife, Drum and Spit Band suddenly disappeared. 'Mammy, where has Uncle Kevin gone?" asked one little girl.
Martin McNulty's description of what happened was wide-eyed and brief. "The Main street swallied us up," he said. The tunnelers claimed in court that they were digging out foundations for a Temperance Hall when a fife, drum and spit band fell on them. You wouldn't really know who to believe. The Fresh Soil Flying squad is monitoring the level of peoples' flower-beds and window-boxes. "Those tunnelers have to put their soil somewhere," they said. The Squad is also making spot checks on peoples' fingernails.
If you live near a bank you're asked to note very carefully the sound of your footsteps as you walk across the kitchen floor. If there's a hollow ring you're asked to contact Dublin Castle.
The Church has given a guarded welcome to the illicit tunnelling. "While we don't agree with its objectives. We heartily approve of the side-effects."
There has been a sharp decline in marital infidelity amongst people who live in bungalows and single-storey dwellings. You can't possibly relax when any

second somebody is likely to come busting up through the floor.
Proper order.

The Chap Didn't Hear A Word...

The man was telling me how brilliant he is at it. He just looks into people's eyes and he can read their character. He was talking and talking and talking and when I tried to say something to him, he hadn't got the slightest interest. I was browned off and bored stiff until a sudden lovely thought struck me I can say anything I like to this guy. He's so utterly into himself and what he's saying that I can have myself a ball.
"Sometimes I think that I'm a rabbit. My nostrils start to twitch and I sniff around outside vegetable shops for loose leaves of lettuce. One man fired at me with his shotgun and nearly blew my powder-puff off." I thought this was a fairly interesting disclosure. How many times do you meet someone on a bus who believes that they are a born-again bunny? He didn't even react. He was now onto his grandfather who could look at the back of peoples' ears and locate where the block was in their energy flow. So I tried him again.
"My uncle Jessie was a gradually diminishing man. He kept removing bits of himself and feeding them to the ducks in St. Stephen's Green. Most of his internal organs were gone by the time he was fifty." I thought this was a fascinating piece of news. I even said it slowly.
"The ducks had enjoyed his appendix and his pancreas

but last week he fed them his thyroid gland and it gave them acute dyspepsia and heartburn." Your man couldn't have cared less. Communication to him was obviously a one-way thing.

I turned off my hearing aid. I was raging I hadn't thought of that before. I turned it off and hummed Glen Miller's "In The Mood" secretly in my mind. You can nod your head in time to the rhythm and really enjoy yourself. There's absolutely no effort involved yet it looks as if you're still listening because your head is bobbing up and down.

All our buses are now no-smoking areas. I hope that a non-listening area will be next. Special seats for people who have no interest whatsoever in anybody else. They can sit there and talk to each other and they won't have to nod their heads or pretend to be listening or anything. They can still go home and say: "I had this great chat on the bus" and the other person can do the same and they can cancel each other out.

An aunt of mine was telling a neighbour about how the doctors had never seen anything like her tonsils and how they were stuffed and mounted in the College of Surgeons and how medical students came from all over the world with their Polaroids just to get a picture of them. He kept repeating "Is that so?" and "Good Heavens" like a mantra until he was finished his crossword. To the day she died she raved about what a fascinating man he was. She never knew that he had survived in the most terrible arenas of World War Two, had recently undergone open-heart surgery and spoke seven languages fluently. She never asked.

Who Can I Phone After Hours?

I thought it would be a lovely thing to do. Get up early and go down to Dollymount Strand to watch the sun rise. There was only another three hours to go, I was still wide awake in bed and hadn't been to sleep yet. If I fall asleep now, I'm finished because I'll never waken again at five thirty. So who can I ring for a chat? Who can I phone at three o'clock in the morning and say: "I just thought I'd ring up to see how you are."

There should be an insomniacs section in the phone book. Ireland must be full of people who are lying awake trying to think of someone to ring. We should all be listed. I couldn't think of anybody except the Irish Rail number that tells you all the trains from Dublin to Westport. But you can't interact with train times. You can't tell them you're trying to stay awake till five thirty.

I rang my brother in Canada. It cost me a bloody fortune. I asked him if the sun had risen in Ontario yet because I never have a clue when I'm talking to him whether he's having his breakfast or putting the cat out. He said it was ten at night and I asked him which night was that because I never know whether he's in today or tomorrow. He asked me if anything was wrong. He always asks me that when I ring him and I always feel obliged to tell him something. So I said that I had a strangulated hernia. I couldn't think of anything else.

I turned on the light at four o'clock and started to play 'I Spy With My Little Eye'. I began with 'A' and the first thing I though of was 'ash tray'. I couldn't see one anywhere and then I remembered: hell, it's downstairs.

So I had to go down to the kitchen to formally see it because if you're going to cheat there's no point in playing. By the time I reached 'X' I'd been half-way around the house and was totally wrecked.
Whenever my father couldn't sleep he used to listen to trawlers and lighthouse men talking to each other on his short-wave radio. They'd be battling through gale-force tens and fighting off man-eating albatrosses with marlin spikes.
The only things I could find were little high-pitched morse code beep beeps which interacted with my hearing aid and made my eyes water. The sky outside was still dark so I rang my brother back in Ontario, told him that my hernia was better and asked him could he think of anything beginning with 'X' because I was playing 'I Spy' and was badly stuck. He said do you realise what time it is and some of us have got work in the morning so I said good night to him even though I still hadn't got a clue which night he was in the middle of.
It's much less trouble all round to watch the sunset. You don't have to ring Canada or anything.

Did You Ever Get Flashbacks Like These?

I haven't got a clue where they are now. It's my own fault because I didn't keep in touch when we left school. The lads went their way and I went mine.
But suddenly it's a matter of great urgency. I have to track them down and ask them. About Latin flashbacks. I'd hate to think that I'm the only one who is sitting up

in bed at three o'clock in the morning and saying "the sons of Tiberius Gracchus have been carefully trained by their mothers." Then I go back to sleep again.

Some people tremble when they are tense and nervous. Others blink rapidly. I used to get involuntary twitches in my left arm. But over the last month or so, something much more embarrassing is happening. Bits of Latin are coming out and there's nothing I can do to stop them. Last week I got really flustered on the bus because an inspector stood beside me and I couldn't find my ticket. Suddenly I heard a voice which I clearly recognised as my own asking him "Who can doubt that Socrates was unjustly punished?" That wasn't too bad because at least the words came out in English. When the heat is really on I'm in deep trouble. A few evenings ago I was in a night-club and the guy beside me was drunk and aggressive. He was also bigger than me. Suddenly his face was staring into mine and he told me that I needed a hair-cut. Before I could stop myself I was telling him in a loud clear voice that "*Elephanti magna capita et parva crura habent.*" He seemed to sober up for a split second and said "What?" So I translated it for him. "Elephants have large heads and small legs." He thought about it for a few moments and conceded: "I suppose you can't bleedin' argue with that." It was a close thing. If any of the guys who sat in the Leaving Certificate Latin class with me are reading this it is imperative that you get in touch.

Have any of you ever answered your phone with the involuntary phrase "the king gives a golden spur to the horse soldier?" I have and it's not one bit funny. People

don't know how to respond when you say something like that.
The stuff that has come out so far is fairly harmless. It's all about sailors giving flowers to farmers' daughters and the deep sea being the abode of fishes. Yesterday I told a complete stranger that "The legs of the stag are very slender." He said "I wouldn't doubt you." But God alone knows what else is in there. We studied loads of stuff about Roman soldiers and vestal virgins with vases on their heads. There are some things you don't say to a bus inspector when you can't find your ticket.

The Lady And The Vamp

It wasn't my fault that she had her neck bitten. God knows, I did my best for her. "Don't go! Don't go round to his place for dinner ... he's really a vampire!" I was shouting at the top of my voice, but it didn't seem to make the slightest bit of difference. I don't know how she could have been so thick. Her best friend had just died from massive nocturnal loss of blood. Two perfectly matching fang bites on her neck. And what does she do? Straight around to the Count's castle for a bit of dinner.
"Don't go in! He only wants you for your neck!" I was yelling at the television for all I was worth. The girl was asking for trouble. How any red-lipped, ample-bosomed, well-brought up youngster can sit down for dinner in her best dress surrounded by live rats and musty cobwebs is beyond me. I was purple in the face at

this stage. "Don't let him kiss you goodnight! Watch out for his teeth!" My nieces and nephews had never seen me so agitated before. It didn't seem to matter to them that any minute now the poor girl was about to join the ranks of the undead. "Behind you! Behind you!"

Poor Count Dracula didn't know where he was from one minute to the next. Just when he had a tasty dinner firmly in his sights, the kindly professor with the foreign accent struck a lump of garlic into his face and he changed into a bat. The poor count couldn't relax for a second. There he was in your woman's bedchamber with the mist swirling around him and the wolves howling Grace before Meals outside. She was sound asleep with her lace nightdress revealing a lovely tasty expanse of neck. The count was licking his lips when the lithe young hero burst into the bedroom and waved a cross in the wretched man's face. There and then he changed into a werewolf, escaped by smashing out through the window and loped away into the mountains without his dinner. I'm not surprised he spent his spare time biting people.

Nobody seemed to need post-traumatic counselling. The kindly professor bumped into his daughter in a graveyard four days after she was buried. She called him "Daddy", embraced him and tried to do a treacherous job on his neck. The lithe young hero couldn't do a thing to help because he was on the floor having problems of his own with a bloodthirsty bat which was really Count Dracula after another of his unexpected turns. "Wave your cross at him! Wave your cross!!"

Thanks be to God they heard me. The girl snarled at her poor Daddy who was immobilising her with a fistful of garlic. Once again the undead were forced to go home without any dinner. Lord Thou art hard on vampires.

Why Ireland Needs A Minister For Outer Space

"Which bit do we own?" the man asked me. "It's about time we sorted it out. The Russians are bangin' up space probes and shuttles and tramplin' all over our bits."
And then he removed his false teeth. "I'll give you a practical demonstration" he said. After warning a couple of women to look the other way, he plopped his teeth into the pint. They sank to the bottom and lay there grinning out through the glass. An old man beside him paled and cancelled his order for a ham sandwich.
"Them teeth," the man said. "Them teeth represent Archimedes and me pint is his bath. Now, by rights the teeth should be leppin' out of the Guinness shrieking 'Eureka' because the level of his pint is after rising. Archimedes displaced his own volume of water in the bath. Me teeth done the same with the Guinness." Which brought him devastatingly to the point. "Every time a new baby is born," he explained. "It displaces its own volume of space. And where does it go? Just like me teeth forcin' the pint upwards, the same thing happens with the space ... up it goes." He said that's how outer space was formed. Almighty God wanted us all to play our part in the act of creation. And he wanted every

country in the world to own a bit of the final frontier And that's where the babies come in.
"Every Irish man, woman and child who ever walked this earth represents a bit of Outer Space which belongs to us," he explained. He said he was more than willing to appear before the League of Nations with his false teeth and his pint to establish our claim.
"What about cats and dogs?" asked a woman who'd been listening to every word.
"Sure each kitten and little pup that gets born in this country sends a bit more space heading up into the atmosphere," he replied.
"What about rabbits and hamsters?" demanded another man. "An . . . an moles and badgers!" yelled the barman. Suddenly everybody in the pub was shouting about canaries and squirrels and ferrets. Suddenly it seemed like we owned the entire universe and everyone was shaking hands and buying rounds, and they all wanted to march on the American and Russian embassies to put the record straight.
"At this very moment" the man announced. "Irish women in the Rotunda and Holles Street are doin' their bit for Mother Eire and Outer Space." So they all decided to march there instead. This raises a powerful new case against contraception.

It's Time To Start Talking To Something

There's so much of it going on that people will believe anything. A man beside me in the bus queue took a little black gadget out of his pocket. He pressed a button and a red light winked. Then he spoke into it. "Remind Verity to activate market gardening expansion phase as soon as Reggie confirms The Antipodes." Then he put it back into his pocket. I felt pathetically ordinary. The only thing I had in my pocket was a Mars bar. Nobody is going to believe you if you start talking into that.

A woman bleeped beside me last week. It's something I'm getting used to. She took a little gadget from her brief-case and checked the readout which suddenly illuminated. "Burmese iron-ore now viable. Go." And she did. Across the road as fast as her legs would carry her.

Once again I felt fierce. Nobody is telling me anything. All these people bleeping and talking into things and driving one-handed because they've got a telephone in the other. You've got to do something. I made a start by talking into fire extinguishers. They could have been made for it. A long tube with a nozzly voicepiece on the end. All you have to do is look official. Stand beside a fire-extinguisher in any large department store. Speak confidently into the nozzle. "Fire office check number B/KL//57764. Extinguisher seven, ground floor, needs a lick of paint; Alert Jeremy." You'll be amazed at the respect you get.

I did it to a pass-machine last week. Put in my card and pressed the buttons. Then spoke very officially into the little slit that dispenses the money. "Co ordinates Y/L/ 893. Valerie won't be in to work tomorrow because she's in bed with the flu. Doctor's note herewith." Then I lodged it in the machine. The woman behind me said

isn't it marvellous what you can do nowadays and she hoped that Valerie gets better very soon.
I was in hospital with asthma about six years ago. They gave me a plastic yoke to blow into. If you blew hard enough three little balls hovered inside it. Good for your lung-power. I taped it to my chest so that it was hidden inside my pyjama-jacket and dangled the tube out through one of my buttonholes. If anybody spoke to me I handed them a message on official hospital notepaper. "This patient is on medication with powerful side-effects. He is temporarily traumatised. Please speak to him in a loud clear voice through his nozzle." Hundreds did.

Get Thee To A Sleepery

There's no place in the city centre it can be done. Last week I was dying to have a rest, but it wasn't easy. I had two hours to put in before meeting a friend. I'd been writing the previous night and hadn't slept a wink. All I wanted to do was lay my head down and snooze for an hour or so. But where? There's nobody to call you in a cinema. And you can't say to the man who tears the tickets: "Would you give us a shout at 6.30?" That's not part of his job specification. People would only start asking him for toast and coffee as well and there'd be no end to it. If you go into a pub, buy a drink and then rest your head on the table for a snooze you'll get a bad name... "I seen your man last week and he was paralytic. .. slumped over his table. . .empty glass. . . not a move out of him." Lying down under the statues is just as bad and benches in parks or railway stations are no better. The market is wide open for Dublin Corporation to build 'Fir' and 'Mná' Sleeperies. Gaily coloured buildings with yellow and green striped walls and flags fluttering on the roof. Each Sleepery will be supervised by a Hammock Warden. Beds would not be popular because you never know what you'd catch. So each Sleepery will sell inexpensive, disposable hammocks.

You will attach these to special hooks which will incorporate a time switch. The warden puts your money in and sets the hooks which act as sleep meters. Then you can climb in and fall asleep. As soon as your time is up, the hammock trembles gently. This is your 30 second warning. If you're not up before the trembling stops, your hammock will pitch you out onto the floor. Or you can insert more money and turn over for another snooze.

Hammock wardens shall use their discretion about distribution of plastic bags. Should a person wish to remove their shoes before sleeping, the warden shall reserve the right to plastic bag their feet. Similarly, should a person require a story before falling asleep the warden shall be the one who selects it. Otherwise you wouldn't be up to some of the yarns that people would want to hear.

Gift vouchers will also be on sale. So you can present your loved one with ten hours of sleep in a Corporation hammock to be taken whenever they feel like it. There shall be no Executive or First Class in the Sleeperies. Public Conveniences work perfectly well without them. And anyway, sleep is a great leveller.

Wild Thrills Of Cricket

A lot of people don't know the first thing about it. A lot of people think that cricket is deadly boring. What they need is something exciting to watch. Like a little bit being cut off the end of the bat everytime the batsman fails to score a run. The umpire takes a hacksaw out of his white coat and waves it to the crowd.
"He didn't score a run that time-what will I do?" And the crowd roars back: "Cut a bit off his bat!" So unless there is a steady flow of runs the batsman finds himself holding an ever-diminishing bat. It serves him right.
There are usually two batsmen at the wicket. This means that the other nine team members are scratching themselves in the pavilion. Doing absolutely nothing. In future they shall be seated on horseback in team corral. Holding lassoes. At regular intervals a loud-speaker shall announce open season on one of the fielders. They are usually scratching themselves as well. Suddenly they'll be forced to scatter as their opponents thunder onto the pitch and do their best to lasso a named fielder. If he is roped he has to leave the pitch as a hostage. This is only fair because if the batsman is holding a diminishing bat it evens things up if the opposing team is diminishing as well.
When one batsman is facing the bowler, the other batsman is standing at the other end. Only marginally involved in the action. In future he shall hold a shotgun. His job will be to try and blow the ball to bits as soon as it leaves the bowler's hand. If he scores a direct hit his team shall get a bonus of fifty and the bowler will get a new ball.

The bowler always tries to hit the stumps with the ball. These are set into the ground. In future if the umpire senses that the crowd is getting restless he shall call for the Stumps Hat. This will be a helmet with the three stumps set onto the top. The batsman shall wear it on his head. Seconds before the ball is bowled the umpire shall shout "GO!" and the batsman will be free to run for his life. This will give the television commentator something to get excited about. It will also give the bowler a moving target.

In future when a bowler shouts, "Howzat?" and the umpire replies, "Not Out"; the crowd can roar, "Oh yes he is!" and the batsman can yell, "Oh no I'm not!" and a lovely argument can start involving everyone in the arena. That way nobody at all is left scratching themselves.

How Is Your Fluffy Rating?

It really does sort out the men from the boys. You put in your fifty pence and you get six goes. You're standing on the pavement outside a shop. Behind the glass front is an infinite number of fluffy toys. Cuddly teddy bears, roly-poly rabbits with spotty waistcoats, coloured penguins and you've got six attempts with the crane to haul out as many as you can. You are putting your manhood on the line and you're doing it in public.

The guy was wearing a leather jacket with 'Anthrax' on the back. His girlfriend was standing beside him. "Anto — get the blue teddy with the pink jacket." He was peering intently at the crane. Concentrating on getting the red penguin.

"Shut up, Sandra," he hissed out of the side of his mouth. "Let me play my own game."

Suddenly he pressed the yellow button which made the crane move downwards. It closed around the red penguin and began to inch back upwards. Anto's eyes were glittering with triumph. The crane gave a little shudder and the penguin fell back down again.

"Now look what you made me do Sandra," he hissed "How can I concentrate on my performance with you talking about blue teddies at the crucial moment?"

Muller is the undisputed king of the Northside. When he approaches the fluffy toy machine in Fairview, people stand back. His average score is two teddies, three rabbits and one penguin for fifty pence. His girlfriend says nothing. Her bedroom is crammed with fluffies. Heaped up on the windows, stuffed into cupboards, shoved in under the bed.

Her mother has warned her: "Daddy says either you stop filling the house up with them teddies or you move out and get a flat." She has explained to her Mammy that Muller is riding a winning streak. If he stops now he might lose his touch.

I haven't yet reached the confident stage where you hitch up your sleeves and casually inspect the fluffies before you start. Muller has taken me under his wing and is giving me hints and tips on technique. "Keep your eye on the teddy ... keep your feet slightly apart ... try and grip the rabbits under their armpits ... don't listen to your girlfriend ... use your first two goes to loosen up the pack ... pick your penguin and GO FOR IT."

This week Muller's tuition paid off. One fifty pence yielded three mice and a fluffy blue whale. The guy beside me snorted dismissively: "Some people have all the luck."

Thank God I had the confidence to say to him: "Luck doesn't enter into it ... you're talking about cool judgement, superior skill and iron nerve."

Muller would have been proud of me.

Give It To Uncle Pat

All I wanted was a quiet game of football with my nephew. David in goal between two trees and me proving that Uncle Pat had never lost it. Hammering in powerful shots like Ian Rush and John Aldridge. Just me and David. That way there'd be no one to tackle me and I'd hardly have to run at all.

"'Scuse me Pat-can I play too?" I don't know where he came from. I told him that he could join in on condition that he kept passing the ball to me and I took all the shots. He had to agree because we owned the ball.

Two little girls were next. "Can we play as well Pat?" I explained the rule which clearly stated that I scored all the goals. "That's not fair" one of them protested. I should have seen her coming a mile off. "I want to score goals as well and so does Gillian." That was when the little boy dug in his heels. "If the girls are going to score goals, we have to pick teams 'cos then we all have an equal chance." That's what I was afraid of. Once you start playing as teams you have to run and people tackle you and you're wrecked after thirty seconds.

The little boy said that me and him would play against the two little girls and David could be in goal. I made it patently clear to him that he was to do all the running on our team. I would be the striker. His job was to chase, tackle, forage and run rings around the girls. I would stand still and conserve all my energy for when he passed the ball to me and I sent an unstoppable rocket past the keeper.

The plan would probably have worked just fine if two more boys hadn't shown up, closely followed by three more girls. The teams seemed to grow and grow and nobody was passing the ball to Uncle Pat. Little girls hacked the legs from under little boys. Vanessa put in the boot with a vehemence that terrified me. One boy rolled around in agony clutching his shin while Elaine jumped over his body and unleashed a rocket which whammed against Matthew's stomach. He hit the ground shrieking that she had done it on purpose. Andrew claimed a penalty on the grounds that Rory's sister had broken his leg when he wasn't looking. Matthew claimed a penalty because all of a sudden he wasn't able to stand up any more.

Grainne wanted a free kick because somebody had stuck their fingers into her eye and she was straight telling her mother. David paced up and down between the two trees yelling at everybody to form a wall. But nobody did. They shrieked at one another and rolled around on the grass clutching their injuries. So me and David took our ball and went home. You have to keep your dignity when you're an uncle.

Soon Every Country In The World Will Copy Us

It seems like a great idea. Nathan Quixby thought of it one night. He was out walking with his wife when a car pulled up and the driver asked him: "How can we get from the N80 to the N11?"
Nathan's wife thought that he was talking in knitting patterns. "Knit one, purl one, then cast off." she said. The American in the car was wide-eyed.
"How in the name of God will that get me to Wexford?" ... "Easy Hiram," said his wife. "The lady thinks you're knitting a sweater."
"God Almighty," he thundered. "I ain't got no needles."
"It'll be very hard so," said Mrs. Quixby.
Nathan thought about the encounter afterwards. Foreign tourists confusing Irish people with Ns and numbers. One man in Tinahely believed that an overseas couple were speaking in Honours Geometry. He even sent into the house for a compass and a set square.
"Don't worry about a thing," he assured them. "My son will have your right angles bisected in no time at all."
"Sacre bleu," said a Frenchman. "Mama Mia," said his wife. She was from Naples. The car took off so fast that two hens never knew what hit them.

Nathan Quixby approached Bord Failte with his idea. Lengthy discussions followed. "We'll use Athlone as our base," he explained. "And we'll paint continuous coloured lines from there to all the major towns and cities." He said that we'd give visiting motorists a colour code. "If you want to drive to Galway you follow the blue line. Dublin is green, Cork is red, and so on." Bord Failte thought it was powerful. You paint an unbroken yellow line from every landing point in Ireland to Athlone. So whether you arrive by air or sea, all the yellow lines lead to the one place. Then you simply consult your colour code.

"Supposing," asked a begrudger, "supposing you happen upon the red line to Cork in the middle of nowhere. How would you know which direction is which?"

But Nathan was up to him. "We paint arrows parallel to the line. They always point away from Athlone."

And the job was right. Bord Failte have bought the paint and appointed the painters. But their identities are being kept secret. This was also Nathan Quixby's idea. He said there were those who would offer inducements. People who would maybe own a pub or restaurant 20 miles or so off the coloured line.

"Could ye ever see your way to sort of painting a detour ... like ... we'll supply the paint and everything." Some people will do anything to get a bit of passing trade.

In future you'll need a government permit to buy a paint brush.

The Drills Are Alive

The workmen weren't convinced. "Pneumatic drills have always made this noise," they explained to Nathan Quixby. "People more or less expect it." Quixby's mind was already working overtime. "You'll never get our workmen to wear leotards," protested a Corporation official. Nathan explained that nothing was further from his mind. "Neither will they be expected to prance around the barrels wearing tutus," he said. "The whole esoteric effect begins and ends with the drill."

Later that week the new Quixby enhanced pneumatic drill made its debut in Capel Street. The operative took up his stance and switched on. He wore a heavy disguise as agreed with his trade union. The drill neither shuddered nor filled the street with deafening decibels. It gently beguiled the workmen instead with a mesmeric rendition of 'The Dance of the Sugar Plum Fairy'. "Thanks be to God we're all well disguised," said the foreman as a crowd gathered to listen. A music critic from a national daily made notes while the workmen further obscured their faces whenever possible with their shovels.

When the drill was switched off the lads braced themselves for a withering broadside of remarks from the gallery. The spontaneous applause was so loud and sustained that they bowed shyly and mentally drafted letters of apology to Nathan Quixby. One or two onlookers threw flowers and one old lady asked if they did requests. "Will you please drill a bit of Vivaldi for my

husband, my children, Auntie Monica and anyone else who knows me?" she asked.
Next morning a crowd had already gathered before the lads arrived for work. Some of the onlookers were reading the reviews in the morning papers. An excited hush descended as the foreman stepped out of the hut and announced: "Ladies-and gentlemen, will you please give a big Capel Street welcome to Anto on the drill who is going to do for you our very own arrangement of 'The Dance of the Sugar Plum Fairy' accompanied by the lads on teaspoons and shovels".
Gardai were drafted into the area to handle crowd-control as Anto and the lads raised the 'Sugar Plum Fairy' to heights undreamed of by orchestral limitations. Shortly before their teabreak the foreman announced that as soon as Anto's drill was further modified, they would be in a position to do requests. The lads no longer wore their disguises and were already whispering among themselves about a national tour with tee-shirts, roadies and merchandising. Their run in Capel Street had been extended to the end of November. Proper order.

Which Department Store Will Be First?

He stood there for ages. Watching the display in the jeweller's window. Glass shelves filled with rings and bracelets. Moving on a carousel. The same circular motion as a mill-wheel. Shelves moving up up up … over the top … then slowly down again. Nathan Quixby's

eyes sparkled. "Why not!?" he exclaimed to the woman standing beside him in the street. She completely misunderstood and gave him six good reasons — all of which involved her husband and a baseball bat.
Quixby brought his vision of the future to one of the largest department stores in Dublin. "Just look," he said. "Hundreds of shoppers all going up escalators to the floor of their choice." The manager rubbed his hands together and beamed. "God is good," he said. Quixby paced up and down excitedly. "That's all very well," he agreed. "But imagine if you can, the floor of your choice coming down to you ... the whole store can operate like a carousel. You actually board your floor at ground level and off you go."
Next day Quixby addressed a meeting of the directors and showed them a chart. "The departures area can be here ... just inside the front entrance. All of the floors shall stop here so that shoppers can board them." He explained that a girl with a nice clear voice can make the announcements. "Clery's are happy to announce the arrival of the fourth floor ... furniture, carpets and curtains now boarding at Gate One." One of the directors licked his lips. "We can even introduce a duty free shopping floor because in a sense our customers are leaving the ground for a while" he said. Quixby nodded. "Now you're talking" he agreed. "And you can display the estimated times of arrival and departure for each floor at ground level."
The Quixby plan for security at nighttime was simple and dramatic. "When the store is empty and everybody has gone home you switch the whole building over to

full speed ahead and all your floors whizz around so fast that you've got supersonic security." He suggested that the same thing could be done once every day. "You could advertise it as "Thrill Seekers Shopping Hour." One director was worried about losing customers who were afraid of flying. "No problem" said Nathan. "We use the Quixby Video Window Plan. Every single window in the store shall show a street level panorama at all times ... buses and pedestrians and red and white barrels. You can even hire stereo headphones and hear cars beeping."

Meanwhile, real passers-by at street level shall see a different window display to think about Carousel Shopping. They better hurry up because Quixby is already working on something else. An inflatable floating tunnel to link Dublin with Liverpool. There is simply no stopping this man.

Are You Ready World?

The audience never knew what hit them. They had paid their money to hear a poetry reading. Suddenly Nathan Quixby's voice boomed through the speakers. "Are you ready to boogie?"

Nobody said a word. So Quixby repeated the question. "I said ... is everybody ready to really get down and get with it?" One man nodded his head because he hadn't got down and got with anything at all since he'd strained his back lifting a gas cylinder two years ago. His wife scarified him with a look. Everyone else stared straight ahead and kept their thoughts to themselves.

The theme from '2001-A Space Odyssey' filled the hall as a Mid Atlantic voice announced: "And now, directly over your heads we bring you The Curiously Quixby World Poetry Tour." Those who did look up blessed themselves hurriedly as the poet in question whizzed along underneath a tightrope. He was attached to it by a safety harness and was reciting as he whizzed: "I come from haunts of coot and hern, with poems and verse and odes, please don't anyone leave your seats, as my smoke device explodes."

At that moment billowing clouds of white vapour poured from under his armpits. "Holy God," shouted a member of the audience. "He's after evaporating and we haven't heard a decent poem yet."

Those who were hoping for recitations about flowers in vases and sunrises over verdant valleys were deeply disappointed as Quixby spun on his harness high above their heads and declaimed: "Half a pound of tupenny rice, half a pound of putty, add a spoon of powdered cement, and solidify a butty."

"That's not poetry," yelled an outraged woman who had never seen smoke pouring from a poet's armpits before. "Stand on a podium and give us 'The Daffodils'." But Quixby went one better. He interacted lyrically with an inflated cow which was whizzed along the rope so that it stopped beside him. "Bovine, oh bovine, fully inflated cow, with this darning needle, I shall deflate thee now." He burst the cow with a bang and six people demanded their money back.

"We didn't pay good money to get a crick in our necks watching the likes of that," they protested. The girl in the paybox promised that Mr. Quixby's best was yet to come and they said that's what they were afraid of. She said it involved three maids a milking, two ban-gardai a bouncing, one Nathan Quixby reciting and a trampoline. By the time that Quixby reached that point his audience had dwindled down to two old women who kept chanting: "Please burst another cow, Mr. Quixby — we loved that bit."

The Quixby World Tour may yet break even on the sale of the teeshirts.

What a Way to Travel

He wasn't getting married. He wasn't even bringing a football team down the country. But Nathan Quixby still wanted to hire a bus. "It's the perfect way of bringing the cat down to the vet's," he explained to Mrs. Quixby. "We can put his litter tray on the top deck and his saucer of milk at the bottom of the stairs and we can make nice 'pish wishing' noises through the driver's microphone."

Mrs. Quixby said be sure to hire a double decker with lots of emergency exits. She still hadn't forgotten the trauma in the taxi.

They had been passing Fairview Park when the cat exploded out of the cardboard box in a blur of flailing claws. It wrapped its front paws around the back of the taxi driver's neck and clung on for dear life. He had screeched to an emergency stop, shouted, "Merciful

Hour," flung the door open and taken off across the park with the cat still attached to the back of his jacket. Mr. and Mrs. Quixby had raced along behind him shouting, "Can we have our cat back please?" A double decker bus seemed like a much better idea.

Nathan never found out how the word got around. The woman down the road rang him and asked "have you got room in your bus for Verity my budgie? She's got droopy feathers and needs creative counselling." The man next door booked a seat for his red setter who kept chasing his tail until he was so dizzy that he had to lean against the leg of a table to stay upright. By the end of a very busy day, the Quixbys had booked every single seat on their bus and were wondering if they could afford to hire a single decker as well to take the overflow. The driver of the green Dublin bus was quite unprepared for the sight that met his eyes when he pulled up outside Maison Quixby. He hadn't seen a woman holding a hen since his summer holidays in Dingle, in 1957. Dogs with bandages wagged their tails, cardboard boxes pulsed and bulged with life as cats did their best to claw their way out to freedom. A white rabbit in a cage kicked its back legs wildly and behaved as if it was having Karate flashbacks.

People at bus stops held out their hands and watched wide-eyed as a bus full of struggling wild-life sailed past. The driver announced that if the woman in the red hat didn't control her hamster it could get out and walk. A canary called Sybil flew out of an open window and was never seen again. The woman with the hen proclaimed a miracle cure because it had just laid an egg in her lap.

The driver said that as soon as he got back to the garage he was going to resign and then volunteer for front line service in the next available world war. Mrs. Quixby poached the miracle egg for her tea.

Would You Live Next Door To A Saint?

It took him completely by surprise. One minute everything was normal. Then the flock of sparrows appeared. Nathan Quixby looked over his shoulder and there they were ... swooping and wheeling behind him. He tried shouting "Shoo!" and "G'way outta that!" but it was no use. The birds followed him around for the rest of the day. He was refused admission to his favourite pub at lunchtime. "I'm sorry Mister Quixby ... one little dog, perhaps ... but a flock of bleedin' sparrows ... it's as much as me job is worth to let that lot in here."
Quixby couldn't understand it. He wasn't throwing breadcrumbs or anything. He wasn't encouraging them at all. "You can come on the bus Mister Quixby — I've no objection to that. But there's no way them birds is gettin' on as well." So Nathan Quixby sat at the back of the bus looking out at the sparrows who flew along keeping perfect pace behind it. They had now been joined by a motley assortment of crows, seagulls and pigeons. "That lot will eat you out of house and home Mister Quixby," said the driver as Nathan alighted at his stop and trudged homewards followed closely by his new found flock. He did his very best to look as if they weren't with him at all.

It was something a little boy shouted that made Quixby look over his shoulder. "Daddy, why are all those rabbits and squirrels following Mister Quixby?" Nathan couldn't believe his eyes. The little animals were streaming out of St. Anne's Park and scurrying along behind him. It was just like a holy picture he'd seen once but he tried not to think about it. "Hail to thee Nathan Quixby," said an old woman. "Peace be with your rabbits." Quixby's reply was unprintable. He slammed the front door behind him and had a stiff drink while the menagerie settled down for the night on his front lawn. It had been joined by an impressive number of stray dogs and tom cats. Next morning Quixby was almost afraid to pull back the curtains. But he couldn't ignore the hymns. A group of old women stood on his front lawn holding lighted candles and singing "Nearer My Lord To Thee." He raced to the bathroom window and looked out. His back garden was like a donkey sanctuary. The parish priest was guarded in his comments. "Let us not be premature about this. We can't beatify a man because his garden is full of tom cats." Quixby said that he didn't want to be beatified thank you very much because he'd never get the oul wans off his front lawn. Pilgrims were now coming from the surrounding parishes and Quixby's next-door neighbour who owned a Mister Whippy van was making a fortune. "It's a miracle Mister Quixby," he said. "That's what it is … a miracle." Nathan Quixby went upstairs, knelt by his bed and prayed for one.

Now You Need Never Go Bald Again

Men don't like to lose it. When their hair is gone, many of them like to put something in its place. Often you look at an old derelict building and you see luxuriant growths of grass and weeds sprouting out of the brick-work. There's only the merest hint of soil yet the wild growth seems to thrive. Nathan Quixby made a mental note and whispered "Verily in sooth" under his breath. Next day he was sitting behind a bald man on the bus. Carefully studying the contours on the shiny cranium. He couldn't help noticing several little dinges ... natural grooves which cried out to be packed with soil. Nathan tapped the man on his shoulder. "Excuse me, how would you like an explosion of new growth on top of thy noble head?"

The man nodded. "But where would you get it Mister Quixby?" he asked sadly.

"Call around to this address and bring some fresh soil," answered Quixby and he handed the man his new business card: *'Quixby Cranium Reclamation — Heads Landscaped by Appointment. Bring your own soil'.*

The man sat patiently in a chair while Quixby eased fresh earth into his dinges. Then he liberally sprinkled the soil with grass seed. He delicately ran a miniature garden roller up and down to flatten the seed. Then he switched his hair-dryer to a very low jet and played it on top of the head. Some of the seed blew away. "Your head is now fertile and the remaining seed has fallen on good ground," murmured Quixby. "Sprinkle it three times a day with a watering can and whenever possible stand out in the rain. You might get the odd dandelion but this is only to be expected."

Quixby received a panic-stricken phone call one week later. "What are ye after doin' to me Mister Quixby? Me entire head is covered with grass!" "Praise the Lord," whispered Nathan fervently. "Any dandelions?" "What am I goin' to do Mister Quixby? A couple more weeks and I'll have a meadow." he stammered.

Quixby advised him to weed the area diligently and call back in a fortnight. "I'll measure you up for a lovely little garden gnome."

After an initial adverse reaction to the notion of head landscaping, Quixby is now unable to keep up with the demand. Suddenly grassy heads are high-fashion and people of both sexes are openly flaunting their manicured lawns up and down Grafton Street. A subdivision of Quixby Enterprises is marketing tiny bird tables and superbly scaled-down miniature lawn-mowers. Quixby himself has shaved his head and sports a healthy harvest of wheat. "I've almost grown enough to bake a biscuit," he said yesterday.

Hairpiece manufacturers are now marketing artificial grass wigs. Wouldn't you know it.

Were You Invited To This Party?

He knew that she was speaking English. But he couldn't identify the dialect. The woman was sitting behind Nathan Quixby on the bus and speaking in a very loud voice. "Morjorie had a gorgeous porty on her potio lost night. She has a seventy-five foot gorden." It was only when he got home that Quixby cracked the code. Put an "a" in place of an "o" and suddenly you've got it. The woman's friend Marjorie had obviously held a gorgeous party on her patio and her garden is a prodigious length. Nathan Quixby felt sad and just a little bit socially deprived. He hadn't got a patio. He was seldom if ever invited to social happenings and the few times that he was, they were never referred to as "porties". He had never dined in the sort of restaurants where "portner had the chilled orange sauce storter which cost £3.50 a drop". It was time to 'upmorket' the Quixby image.

He worded his invitations very carefully. "Nathan Quixby has great pleasure in inviting you to a porty on the potio which he hasn't got. You are requested to bring your own paving stone. When speaking to other guests on the night, kindly substitute "o" for "a" at all times."

Society circles were agog. Nobody had ever given a party on a non-existent patio before. The notion of trundling your paving stone to a party in a wheelbarrow was just too exciting. And bit by bit it happened. Huge gaps began to appear in Dublin pavements. Corporation officials couldn't figure it out. At first they thought it might be street artists who were bringing their work home with them. Then they suspected environmental activists from the newly formed "Let The Worms Breathe Movement". But their investigations drew a complete blank. Then they ran a computer check on all recent purchases of wheelbarrows and crowbars. Meanwhile Quixby cleared his back-yard of old bikes and bags

of coal and worked around the clock making banana sandwiches.
The night of the party was moonlit and clear. Socialites with dress-suits and wheelbarrows converged on Quixby's house while his neighbours watched from behind their curtains. They whispered that it must be a nightclub bouncers' union meeting with a wheelbarrow race afterwards.
The work of laying the patio began. Paving stones were humped out from wheelbarrows and sibilant hisses of agony rent the air. Eyes watered and guests walked gingerishly like John Wayne. "Alert the hernia unit," said Quixby into his phone to the nearest hospital on call. Fleets of ambulances with blue flashing lights ferried the guests away into the night. They were closely followed by Dublin Corporation lorries filled with the missing paving stones. Quixby eyed the mountain of banana sandwiches and shook his head. "Porty on the potio how are ye." he said.

Are You Green And Friendly?

She was American, young and beautiful. A famous television star. She told Gay Byrne quite definitely that Ireland is very green. Then her voice became charged with emotion. "Everyone is so warm and friendly . . . I feel like I am surrounded by good and true friends. I just looooove Ireland." The studio audience burst into wild spontaneous applause. They overlooked the fact that she hadn't got any Irish relations. You can't have everything.

Nobody in the Late Late studio noticed how she paused at the end of her emotive statement. Almost as if she knew that the applause was coming. Nathan Quixby watched his television approvingly. "Good girl," he murmured. "Now give them phrase three, top of page two." Even as he murmured she brushed away an imaginary tear and spoke softly. "I've only been here for two days yet I feel as if I've come home … it's … it's almost as if I belong." She paused and waited. No applause. "Hold it … hold the pause," urged Quixby. "Now throw in the clincher." The young star looked dreamily into the middle distance. "I'll be back … goodbye Ireland and thank you … I'll be back … that's a promise." The whole place went wild. Quixby nodded and ticked something in his notebook.

The crash-course at Nathan Quixby's "Green And Friendly Academy" only takes one morning. Visiting rock stars learn how to bound onto the stage waving madly at the crowd and yelling "Hello Ireland! Let's go!" Pause for the thunderous ovation. Let it die down a bit. "Me and the boys have been on the road for six months now and this is what kept us going … Ireland. We were just saying to Bono … man — you just gotta get us a gig in Dublin … our soundman is Irish … Kevin . DO YOU WANNA ROCK IRELAND?" — The whole place explodes. Nathan Quixby stands at the back and murmurs: "Nice one … don't forget to hit them with Danny Boy … lots of guitar feedback, nice one."

For a nominal fee you can rent-a-relation while you're here. Most visiting Americans who sign on with Quixby pay for the use of his great-grandfather.

"Honey Quixby ... born in a bothy . . evicted during a blizzard . . . deported to Van Diemen's Land, escaped, arrived home during the Famine, survived, went steerage class on the Titanic, rescued, fought alongside General Custer, adopted by the Indians, became Big Chief Honey Quixby, taught jigs and reels to the Cherokee nation, died tragically when a totem pole fell on him."

Quixby's greatgrandfather never left Ballyhaunis. "But it's green and he was always friendly," stressed Nathan. And he paused. And waited.

Things That Go Hop In The Night

It wasn't Nathan Quixby's fault that he was riddled with fleas. When he took in the stray kitten he didn't know that he would be invaded. Little by little he began to wriggle and squirm and scratch. Little by little the people who sat beside him on the bus did the same. When he went to the cinema he became the epicentre of a writhing mass of people who took off their jackets and raked each others backs with their fingernails. " No offence Mister Quixby," said the cinema manager. "But would you ever get yourself sprayed or fumigated or something."

Nathan Quixby was sitting up in bed combing his body with a wire brush when a faint memory began to stir in his mind, something about a Wild Life book he'd once read about foxes. When a fox is swarming with little hoppers it takes a ragged piece of sheep's wool in its mouth and slowly backs its way, tail first, into a river.

The fleas keep moving forward to get away from the water and take refuge in the lump of wool as a last resort. The fox then releases the wool which floats away down river and all its troubles are over.

"Begod Martha-that is it! I need a lump of sheep's wool," he said but his wife didn't hear him. She had taken to sleeping downstairs on the sofa in an outsized plastic bag. Quixby looked at his watch. "Good," he said. "Two o'clock in the morning. All the sheep will be asleep." He drove out into the countryside and traumatised a sheep by chasing it around a field with his wife's scissors.

It was three o'clock in the morning when Nathan drove onto Dollymount Strand. He undressed in the car and began to walk down to the water's edge backwards. A white-faced girl watched wide-eyed from inside her boy-friend's van. "Marty," she gasped. "There's a man out there in his pelt and he's walking backwards." Marty had a quick look to make sure it wasn't his girl-friend's father. Then he stared again.

"Don't look Natalie," he cautioned. "Whatever he's doing, he's got a huge lump of wool in his mouth." Suddenly Quixby began to scratch vigorously. "That does it Natalie. The man has no shame. Lock both the doors when I get out." Marty approached Quixby with wide circling movements. "Stand well clear!" shouted Nathan as he eased himself backwards into the Irish Sea. "I'm only lepping with fleas".

Five minutes later the two men stood side by side watching the lump of wool floating away towards

Liverpool. "Did I ever tell you about foxes?" asked Quixby and they both lit a cigarette.

Don't Sit On Your Glasses

People are always doing it. Sitting down on top of their reading glasses. They also walk on them and twist their spectacles out of shape.

"Aversion Therapy is your answer," suggested Nathan Quixby. "I propose to open a clinic filled with chairs. A pair of glasses will rest on each of them. If anybody attempts to sit down, the chair will zap ten thousand volts through their system." Mrs. Quixby pointed out patiently to her husband that people are not going to pay good money to have themselves riddled with electricity every time they sit down. "You can stick a knitting needle into a socket and get the very same effect free of charge," she said. Quixby nodded.

Nathan kept his next plan to himself. A magnetic field which operates at ceiling level. If you leave your glasses on a chair or lying on the floor, they simply shoot straight up to the ceiling. You stand up on the diningroom table or shin up a stepladder to get them back down again. He should have explained it to his wife.

Mrs. Quixby rang the parish priest and told him that she had a sudden outbreak of the paranormal in her kitchen. "I want to make a cup of tea but the kettle is stuck to the ceiling. I think it's some kind of passive poltergeists because they're not actually throwing things around." The parish priest dropped in with a bottle of holy water and agreed with Mrs. Quixby that her knives and forks shouldn't be hopping up and down in the kitchen drawer. He said a pious aspiration and opened it. The knives and forks shot upwards to join the kettle on the ceiling.

"Get thee behind me," he said.

Nathan Quixby modified the magnetism so that it only interacted with pairs of spectacles. "Your kettle is no longer at risk, Mrs. Quixby," he said. The parish priest called around later that evening to bless the knives and forks and his spectacles parted company with his body. He watched them floating upwards and suggested that Mrs. Quixby get a synod of bishops round to sort out her kitchen. "It's only magnetism, Father," explained Nathan. "If you wedge your glasses well in behind your ears they won't be able to float."

"Putty is your answer," he told a meeting of the Reading Glasses Federation of Ireland.

"You stick a lump of putty behind either ear and that works as a sort of brake on your spectacles." The acting president said that many of his members are highly fashion conscious and like to wear their glasses hitched up on top of their heads. "One can hardly wedge lumps of putty up there, Mister Quixby," he said dismissively. Nathan told him that you can't have it everyway. Quixby is now perfecting a plan to stop people from accidentally swallowing their hearing aids. There is no putty involved so he is most optimistic.

Ring-a Ring-a Rugby

He was terrified out of his wits. Grown men were grabbing one another with menacing grunts and crunching tackles. Nathan Quixby stood on the touchline at his very first rugby match. He was afraid to make eye contact with any of the players in case they suddenly veered off the pitch and bit him. He hummed 'All Things Bright And Beautiful' to himself as more and more men dived headfirst onto a flailing mountain of arms and legs. It was the only way he could keep his head together.

"My dear gentlemen," murmured Quixby to his training squad. "There will be no snarling or growls of any description. We will start our session this evening by reciting together 'Up The Airy Mountain, Down The Rushy Glen'". The assembled players looked at one another and looked at the ground and shuffled their feet. "That's not the way we do it, Mister Quixby," explained a hulking forward who specialised in baring his teeth and baying at people. "The whole idea is to unnerve the opposition and intimidate them off the pitch." An hour later Nathan's persuasive powers were beginning to bear fruit. "Go!" he commanded and a fifteen stone giant powered along the touchline with the ball under his arm. "Intercept!" shouted Quixby and a defender stepped forward with a lily in his hand. "I offer thee this flower in exchange for the ball because it matches thine eyes."

The attacker stopped dead in his tracks and asked what in the name of God was going on. "Precisely," murmured Quixby. "There are more ways of unsettling a team than baring your gumshields at them." He assured them that Saturday would be an afternoon to remember.

Both teams were warming up on the pitch twenty minutes before the kick-off. Quixby's opponents were punching the air and grunting and grinding at the far end. Gradually they became aware of Nathan's squad merrily putting their hands together and enjoying a cheery 'Pat a Cake, Baker's Man'.

Then the whole team joined hands and swung into a jolly 'Ring a ring a rosy'. The growling faded into an uneasy silence. Players looked at one another but nobody said anything.Twenty minutes into the game, passes went wildly astray as primroses were offered in the scrum and players exchanged recipes for Quiche Lorraine in the line-out. Co-ordination completely fell to pieces when Quixby's full-back caught the ball and stuffed it up his jersey while his teammates hid their hands behind their backs and chanted 'Queenie eye oh, who has the ball?'

After an emergency meeting of the I.R.F.U. it has been decided to either ban Quixby for life or appoint him as the National Coach. Emergency is right.

Spot-The-Hole

He got the idea from Spot-the-ball. "The entire city is riddled with roadworks holes," explained Nathan

Quixby. "There's no reason why you can't use them to make a few bob."
Dublin Corporation listened very carefully. "Take an aerial photo of the next street which is scheduled for the shovel," he said. "Put it onto an entry form and let the citizens of Dublin forecast where the hole will be. They can mark it with an 'X'." There and then the officials of the Corporation passed a unanimous motion which agreed that Quixby's blood was worth bottling. The man was only getting warmed up. "That competition can be for a weekly prize but we need something to really get the punters going wild once a month." His eyes shone as he suggested using an American satellite. "Once a month we can publish a picture of the city taken from a great height and the holes will appear as dots. Each entrant will simply be asked to join up the dots any way that he or she likes and the job will be right." The corporation officials were half afraid to ask Quixby how you selected a winner and when one of them did enquire, he looked pained.
"Sure it's obvious," he said. "Whichever entry most closely resembles a map of the Lord Mayor's digestive system will win the super prize."
His suggestion for cutprice messages was a humdinger. "Bring over a full-blooded Red Indian and let him train the roadworks boys in tom-tom language. That way you can send a message to anywhere in Dublin using the roadworks barrels."
Quixby produced tape recordings which proved that some of the boys were already doing it. The first track he played was a message from the lads on the North

Circular Road to the boys on the shovels up in Harrington Street. "That one's a tip for a dog in the 8.15 at Shelbourne Park," he explained. "This next one is from Marty out in Rathmines to his wife in Kimmage telling her to put his dinner in the oven because his bike is punctured and he'll be late home."

Thanks to Nathan's prompting the Corporation Amateur Dramatic Society is now staging "Ali Baba" at lunch-time beside any roadworks which has got more than forty barrels. Plans are going ahead for laying down artificial grass mats, putting a few poles across the barrels and borrowing horses from friendly Arab States.

"Street theatre has been done before," said Quixby. "But no other corporation in the world has ever put on street horse shows. We can even flood the occasional hole and run inner-city sheep dipping contests."

It's hard to credit that apart from a medal for his confirmation this man has never won a major award.

They'll Never Rob This Bank

"Landmines blow up when you walk on them." That's what Nathan Quixby explained to the top level commission on Total Bank Security. He said that if you mined the area leading to the vaults, the money would be absolutely safe. Especially if nobody knew where the mines were. Not even the bank staff. "A map," he said. "There will have to be a map." This could be in ten sections. Just like a jig-saw. Each section would be tattooed to a Garda's stomach. The vault could only be opened by summoning the ten gardai who would then remove their shirts and stand side by side in the appropriate formation. "Who's going to rob a bank with an arrangement like that?" he asked .

The banks advanced an undisclosed sum to Quixby so that he could research his security plans. He built an experimental bank on the Curragh and mined the area in front of the vaults. That night there was an unmerciful explosion and a further sum was advanced so that Quixby could rebuild his bank. "A mouse," he explained. "A mouse walked on one of my land mines."

When the bank was rebuilt, Quixby suspended cats from the ceiling in canvas hammocks all around the mine-field. Ten gardai volunteered to have their tummies tattooed. Observers from the major banks crouched behind sandbags. They wore tin hats. The siren on the roof was activated to summon the gardai on their bikes. There was a cataclysmic explosion. "In future the cats will be fitted with earmuffs" said Quixby. "The siren freaked them."

As soon as the bank was rebuilt, farmers from the Curragh placed a picket on it. "Our sheep are all up trees and their minds are blown," they protested. Quixby promised that he was now working on non-explosive total bank security. "Kangaroos," he said. "All the paper money in the bank shall be stored in their pouches. Each kangaroo shall be designated 50 square metres hopping room. Nobody in their right mind would raid a bank and drive away a significant number of kangaroos." An extension was built onto to the bank to allow for the required hopping room.

The Union of Bank Officials pointed out that nobody in their right mind would work in an office where you had to lasso a kangaroo everytime somebody wanted to make a sizeable withdrawal. The extension to the bank was knocked down again and the zoo was advised to disregard Quixby's letter of the 3rd inst. But the man was far from finished.
"Boa constrictors eat cows," he said. "Just supposing that the cow had first swallowed a significant sum of money. Now there's security for you. "Merciful hour," said a bank official. He was probably right.

Do Not Attempt This When Alone

He told her to be a slice of toast. The woman in the bus queue was astounded. "God but I feel so depressed." That's what she had told Nathan Quixby. "My life just isn't worth living right now." Quixby explained patiently that the best course of action was to quit her body completely. "Get right out of yourself and into a fantasy," he said gently. "Be a slice of toast."
Before she knew where she was Quixby had her standing in the queue with her eyes closed repeating over and over again with passionate conviction — "I am a slice of toast." He urged her to even greater heights. "Sense into your crust ... become aware of your butter." The woman's face lit up. "Be God I can even feel my marmalade," she whooped and the bus queue broke into spontaneous applause. "Now I want you to joyously pop up out of a toaster," coaxed Quixby and the woman shot into the air with a yell of "Wheee!"

Her transformation was dramatic. The glow had returned to her cheeks and her eyes sparkled. When the bus arrived the conductor announced that nobody was coming on board till they stopped leaping up and down and shouting affirmations. "Is it some sort of voodoo or what?" he asked. Quixby shook his head. "We're all sensing into our crusts and jumping out of toasters," he explained. The conductor shouted to his driver to shut the doors fast and put the boot down before the whole bus was in the grip of toast hysteria. Quixby is quite used to this.

He has revolutionised the treatment of senior citizens aged ninety or over. "It is enough for you to feel even a weak flicker of your former vitality," he explained to his old age therapy group. "Sense into it and let your full awareness dwell on it and you will fan it into explosive life." Then he led Martha Hahesy very gently into her Yamaha 1,000 cc fantasy. The ninety-six-year-old woman straddled a wooden chair in the centre of the group and repeated over and over again: "I am a Yamaha 1,000 cc motorbike". Quixby urged her to sense into her handlebars and exult in her shiny chrome. "Your tank is full Martha — the open road beckons." The old lady began to throb with primitive power.

"Open up your throttle ... give it the gun girl" exhorted Quixby. With a wild swing of her boot Martha kick-started herself and roared around the room. Somebody had the presence of mind to open the door and much to her own amazement Martha Hahesy overtook an Express bus six miles outside Dundalk.

Quixby's only request is that the senior citizens in his group return the chairs. He stresses that none of these fantasies should be attempted while you are alone.
"No slice of toast is an island," he observes and who are we to doubt him?"

Do You Really Know What You Look Like?

He couldn't take his eyes off the backs of her ears. Nathan Quixby was sitting behind her on the bus. He thought they were quite the most exquisite backs of ears he had ever seen. So he told her. "Madam, the backs of thine ears have just awakened in me the kind of lyrical euphoria normally reserved for the great mystic poets." Fortunately she was able to take a compliment. Yet, her response still saddened him. "Thank you very much," she said. "Come to think of it I have never seen them myself."
Quixby stared at the backs of all the heads on the upper deck of the bus and burst, quite spontaneously, into a speech which brought the conductor racing up the stairs.
"How can we ever hope to know each other when we don't fully know ourselves?" asked Quixby. "How many of you have ever seen your feet in their entirety? I call on you now to whip off your shoes and socks and gaze upon the balls of your left and right feet." The conductor announced that he was stopping the bus if anyone as much as loosened a shoelace. But Quixby was only getting warmed up. "If anybody possesses two mirrors let us take it in turn to really get to know the

backs of our heads, the rims of our ears . . . yea-and if the bus is warm enough let us gaze for the first time upon the small of our backs." It was at this stage that the bus shuddered to a halt and Quixby found himself walking. And still thinking.
He called his shop 'Two Mirrors To Know You'. Nobody else had ever thought of selling them on the double as a 'See Your Own Shoulder Blades For The First Time' set. Or 'Take a Voyage of Discovery Around The Back of Your Head'. You could also hire a mirror and sit on the floor to inspect the soles of your feet. Quixby encouraged you to hum 'Getting To Know You' and 'Happy To Make Your Acquaintance' while you did it. The man was only still getting warmed up. Badges which you wear on the back of your jacket were a huge seller. "Very often somebody is sitting behind you and they're not really sure if it's you or not," he explained. "They're a bit shy about tapping you on the shoulder in case they make a mistake." Quixby simply printed your photograph onto a badge which you then wore on your back. There was no stopping the man. "Bald is beautiful," he preached. "Especially if you have your favourite work of art painted onto the region." He gave the lead by shaving his scalp and having 'Dancers In Blue' by Degas handpainted onto his head.
Earstick was next. "Let us double the lipstick market by selling it to both sexes — the rims of our ears are crying out for the stuff." He offers this next manoeuvre absolutely free. No mirrors required. "Close one eye and see for the very first time the other side of your nose." This can be done with impunity upstairs on a bus.

Excitement At Bedtime

"The wind was so strong that you could almost lie back against it."

That's what a woman said to Nathan Quixby. His eyes sparkled and he embraced her. "Madam — thou hast just triggered off a momentous train of thought," he said and rushed straight home to experiment with the hairdryer. It was very easy to keep a feather suspended in mid-air. Then he invited a few friends around with their hair dryers. They sat on the floor and directed the jets of hot air upwards so that they met at a point and supported a table tennis ball.

"We are gradually edging our way towards the ultimate bed," announced Quixby. "Just imagine lying down on your bedroom floor and pressing a button which activates warm air outlets directly underneath you ... very gently you are wafted upwards until you reach the desired height which can be pre-set. Then you sleep in perfect peace."

The lads were thrilled. No more worries about hands reaching out from underneath the bed to grab you. The outlets which support your head can be set slightly higher than the others so you don't even need a pillow.

"And best of all lads," explained Quixby. "You can throw away your alarm clocks because the air jets can be programmed to lower you onto the floor at any time you like. You can even select the severity of the bump."

Quixby and his friends drilled holes in the sitting room ceiling. Then the lads shinned up ladders and directed the nozzles of their dryers through the bedroom floor.

They switched on. Quixby lay down directly above the holes and urged the lads to turn up their jets. Wisps of smoke rose from his clothing and he roared to the boys to switch off before they cremated him. The message was lost in the translation and they increased the intensity. Quixby was forced to make a dash to the showers while the lads stood on top of their ladders and jetted hot air upwards for all they were worth. It wasn't a great night. "What we need now are cylinders of high-powered oxygen," said Quixby and he invited around all his friends who worked as welders and male nurses in chest clinics.

They brought their cylinders with them. Quixby's friends stood on the table and directed the oxygen tubes through the holes in the ceiling. "When I thump the floor I want you to wham up the oxygen," he said through a voice pipe. Then he positioned a saucer of milk on the floor and placed the cat beside it. "Tis a far finer thing you do this night," he said to the cat and thumped the floor with his foot. They never found the saucer. The cat was discovered six gardens away. Quixby still shows his visitors the exit marks which it left en route.

He is now working on the ultimate jacuzzi but his friends refuse to have anything to do with it.

Would You Drink In This Pub?

He got the idea from a cormorant on the Liffey. "I was crossing Butt Bridge when I saw it sleek and black and swimming upstream," said Nathan Quixby. "Suddenly it dived and reappeared thirty seconds later gulping down a fish." It was the unexpectedness of the event that intrigued him. "You really had no idea where the bird was going to come up next." he said. So he called his new pub 'The Cormorant'."

A trap door behind the bar led down to the cellar. This was flooded with warm water almost to the top of the steps. A series of carefully concealed trap doors were set into the floor amongst the tables. These were carpeted over so expertly that you couldn't see the joins. "The basic idea is to stimulate my patrons and give them something to talk about whenever things get a bit dull," explained Quixby.

During such a quiet spell Rufus, the barman, announced in a loud voice "Avast and belay — all of a sudden I feel like a cormorant." Then he stripped down to his Y-fronts and shinned up a step-ladder. With a mighty splash he dived into the cellar which was stocked with all manner of fish. At any time during the next thirty seconds he burst up through one of the secret doors with his body glistening and a fish in his mouth.

Quixby learned from his mistakes. "Initially we didn't tell our patrons anything about it. This was an error of judgement," he confessed. "The first time that Rufus began to whip off his clothes there was a very mixed reaction. Some women roared encouragement such as: "Get them off you!"Others locked themselves into the Ladies and refused to come out. One man placed a plastic shopping bag over his wife's head and eased her under the table."

When the barman shot up out of the floor for the first time, one patron with a weak heart went into immediate bronchospasm while his wife whacked Rufus with her brolly and shouted "Get back down there and come up decent!"
A printed warning card on each table was quite sufficient. "Dear Patron, When you least expect it, the barman is likely to plunge off a ladder and explode up out of the floor beside your table. This is meant to happen. Please feel free to grab the fish out of his mouth and bring it home with you for the dinner."
Quixby is shortly opening his Tarzan Lounge where the barman will wear a loin cloth and periodically launch himself from the counter on the end of a rope. Rufus's brother will perform this task because he can't swim.
"He will shout "EEEEAAAAAAA" and drop a bag of crisps or peanuts onto your table as he swings past" explained Quixby.
There is no cover charge at 'The Cormorant'.

Have You Seen The Ard Feis Gallop?

We've got them already. Training courses which teach you how to talk on radio and television. The indirect insult: "Some people would say you wouldn't know the truth if it bit you." The civilised challenge: "I didn't interrupt you when you were talking so unless you want to waken up with a crowd around you ..."
There's not really much more can be said about full, frank and fruitful exchanges or mutually beneficial

meetings. This is why Nathan Quixby has set up his revolutionary new agency — Up And Down The Steps.
"Arrive and be noticed." This is the first lesson that public figures learn from Quixby. "You are so boring," he explained. "All you ever do on television is get out of cars holding briefcases and walk up steps into grey, unimaginative buildings. Sure, my granny could do that."
So Quixby gives them basic instructions in the 'Brief Case Shuffle.' Out of car, a quick leap into the air clicking the feet together as they do it, a nifty twirl and then soft-shoe shuffle up the steps humming 'New York, New York'.
At first they were a little bit sceptical but the public response to The Ballingarry Boiler Makers' Union soon convinced them. Six delegates fired the national imagination when they arrived at Government Buildings for talks with an independent assessor. They burst across the television screens with a quick excerpt from 'The Pirates of Penzance' and paused to produce white doves from their briefcases before high-kicking their way up the steps and into the building.
The Government switchboards were jammed. "Give these people what they want." That is the message which came through loud and clear from the voters of the nation.
"How do I sit around the table and clinch it?" Lesson two in Quixby's training course.
"The whole country is fed-up looking at the lot of you making pretend notes on your jotters and letting on to

be talking to each other. Do something human for a change."

Once again, Quixby's students were a little unsure. But public reaction to the Knockmealdown Metalworkers clinched it.

As the camera tracked around the seated delegates, one of them produced a placard from under the table and held it towards the lens. "Slippery Lad in the 8.15 at Harold's Cross tomorrow night. It's mine. So I know."

Three other delegates leaned forward and sang "Hello to you Mammy in Ballisodare, Hello Aunty Mavis and Florrie in Clare." Once again the whole country voted with their telephones.

Lesson Three at Quixby's Academy is called the Ard Fheis Gallop. We can't wait.

The World's First Dublin To Galway Swimming Pool

You take out all the seats. This gives you an empty carriage. Then you flood it with warm water. But you don't fill it up to the roof. This would mean that railway passengers would have to swim underwater. CIE were amazed by the simplicity of the idea. It was one of Nathan Quixby's finest. But he overlooked the question of waterproofing the carriage. The world's first Dublin to Galway swimming pool was fine leaving Heuston Station. American tourists splashed up and down quite happily. But by the time they had reached

Athlone everybody was paddling in very shallow water. It was scarcely ankle deep. Too many leaks.
Quixby refilled the carriage to the very top and parked it in a siding. He paced around it tirelessly with a stick of chalk and marked all the leaks. CIE quick-setting putty did the rest. The swimming pool carriage was back in service with a special sliding hatch fitted into the roof. This enabled adventurous passengers to dive in headfirst. A sign was placed beside the hatch. "Passengers are warned not to dive from the roof when the train is in motion — you might get a belt from a bridge." Every time the train stopped at a station the guard sounded the "All Clear for Diving" siren and passengers in bathing togs scrambled up onto the roof. It was a magnificent sight.
Quixby learned from his mistakes. His swimming pool carriage was originally placed at the centre of the train. But the ticket checker complained fiercely. "I have to strip down to me underpants everytime I want to clip their tickets. And how in the name of God am I supposed to get from one end of me train to the other? I'm only worn out with all the swimming." So the waterfilled carriage was moved to the end of the train. The Catering Section thought it was a shame not to put so much water to good use especially as it was salt water from Galway Bay. This is how the fish came to be introduced. Fresh fish for the dining car swimming around in Quixby's carriage. Passengers could alight at any station with a waiter and indicate the fish of their choice through the window. He then shinned up onto the roof and scooped it out with a net. The Catering

Section also wished to introduce crabs and lobsters but Quixby said "steady on lads or you'll empty my pool entirely".
This is the kind of farseeing judgment which sets the man apart. And motivates him to work on his new Limerick to Dublin ice rink. A man apart is right.

How Irish Worms Joined the CIA

It's a very beautiful Irish tradition. You sprinkle flour onto a tray on Mayday and place an earthworm on top of it. As the worm wriggles around it spells out the name of your true love.
Nathan Quixby watched an earthworm in his kitchen spelling out "Samantha O'Reilly" in perfect Celtic script. The man was mesmerised. "I hope that the world is ready for this," he said and he telephoned the American embassy.
A top secret meeting followed during which Quixby outlined his plans to revolutionise cloak and dagger espionage. "Give me a classified code-word and two weeks to train my worm," he said. "At the moment it can only spell "Samantha O'Reilly". The embassy entrusted him with the codeword "Rumblescrumption" which Quixby pointed out would need a very long tray and a kilo bag of flour. Then he went into hiding for a fortnight. Quixby manufactured a wax tray into which he deeply grooved the code word. It was cut into the wax to form a channel which spelt out 'Rumblescrumption'. Then he put the worm into position and activated a tape

which repeated a highly irresistible mating call at the far end of the tray. The worm powered its way along the channel at high speed.
For the next two weeks it wriggled continuously along the groove until it could almost spell the code word in its sleep. The American charge d'affairs was profoundly impressed as he watched the worm inscribing the top secret word with an effortless series of wriggles and an elegant flourish. "The sky is the limit with these little guys," he whooped. "They can burrow into embassies all over the world and the only things we need to de-brief them are a tray of flour and a mating call." Systematic checks have revealed that Irish worms are quick to learn, highly adaptable and can wriggle in any language you care to teach them. At this very moment in embassies as far apart as Moscow and Montenegro, top ranking spies are hunched intently over trays as crucial messages are inscribed in flour. A Russian counter-espionage plot, which involved digging up worms in Tinahely and sending them to Kiev in a diplomatic bag, has so far failed to infiltrate the American network successfully. A Russian-trained worm which surfaced in the US embassy in Cambodia was instantly detected. It wriggled along the de-briefing tray and repeatedly inscribed the name "Samantha O'Reilly'. Nobody knows where this girl lives but the American Intelligence Network owes her a huge debt of gratitude.

When In Trouble Confuse Them...

It's a great way of getting out of awkward situations. Do something totally unexpected. Then run.

A friend of mine was stopped by three muggers in Middle Abbey Street. It was very dark and very late. "What the hell kept you lads?" he snarled. "The Masher won't like this ... we should be in the getaway car by now." They paused and looked at each other. "Where's the cutting equipment?" my friend raged. "It's not one of your ordinary safes ye know." Then he asked which one of them had brought along the forged passports.

"Now look pal," one of them began, "I don't know what the ..."

"Don't you bleedin' 'Look pal' me," stormed my friend. "When The Bone Crusher hears about this he'll whip out your epiglottis with a marlin spike." Then came my friend's finest moment. He suddenly switched roles and dedicated his next song of the evening to Natalie and Darren and everyone in the Harrington Street Hit Squad. Then he walked away towards O'Connell Street holding an imaginary microphone and singing 'From the Candy Store on the Corner to the Chapel on the Hill'. When he got around the corner he ran for his life.

Two years ago my friend woke up at three in the morning. There was somebody moving around downstairs. Very quietly he got dressed. Then he pulled a pair of his wife's tights over his head and shouldered the sack which he always kept beside the bed. Easing his way backwards down the stairs he shrieked — "Ye didn't have to do it ... ye didn't have to chop off Marty's head with a Wilkinson sword... what'll I tell his wife?" Then he raced into the sittingroom where two men stood rigid with shock. "We went up the stairs," he babbled. "An' your man yelled 'Banzai'. Then he whipped off Marty's head with one swipe. Now he's assembling a machine gun."

At this moment my friend's wife started drilling down through the bedroom floor with a Black and Decker drill. "Which one of yez is comin' upstairs with me to sort him out and get Marty's head back?" my friend demanded. "He'll never get a chance to throw the grenades if we rush him first."

The lads didn't even pause to sing 'From the Candy Store on the Corner'. They went out through the sitting room window the imaginative way.

My friend hadn't got any opportunity to try out his contingency plan. The one where he dresses up as a bishop and wanders into the room protesting — "I don't usually do Confirmations at this hour but the Lord works in wondrous strange ways". Then he whips out a stop watch and asks the intruders to name the Seven Deadly Sins in three seconds starting from now. It saddens him deeply that nobody ever sticks around to be confirmed.

Would You Do This In The Back Of A Taxi?

All it took was one enterprising taxi driver. He was fed up sitting in his car for hours reading books. Waiting ... always waiting. Painstakingly inching his way towards the top of the queue at the taxi rank. "There must be some way I can make a few shillings while my car is empty and idle." That's what he thought. But he didn't leave it at that.

Jasper Pringle attached a small two-wheeler trailer to the back of his car. It held two large milk churns full of water. A rubber hose ran from the current churn through the back window of the taxi. He used this to fill up a metal bucket which he heated with a primus stove. Then he put a sign on top of his car. "Step inside and soak your feet for 50p."

The old women with bunions exploding out through their shoes were thrilled. "The blessings of God on ye son," they said. "The feet is only killing us." Then they dumped their parcels on the back seat and kicked off their shoes.

The notion of a bucket full of personalised water was a great selling point. "No offence son but a bunion is a very intimate sort of thing as also is the feet — you wouldn't want to be plunging them into any old bucket."

Jasper Pringle recorded the old ladies sighs of ecstatic relief as they immersed their feet. And he approached passersby at the Taxi rank.

"This is how my clients feel about the unique service in the back of my car," he said. Then he played them the tape.
"What in the name of God are ye doin' in there?" demanded one startled old man.
"We're soaking feet," explained Jasper Pringle.
"That's what they all say," replied the old man. "I think I'd feel safer on the bus."
The other taxi drivers at the rank were quick to cop on. The queue outside Jasper's car included several traffic wardens and off-duty gardai. One driver bought the franchise from Pringle so that he could stand beside the taxi selling perfumed talcum powder. Another one who owned a London cab installed Madame Mystery lingo in the back of his car with her own crystal ball and cups full of tea leaves.
He did a deal with Jasper so that for a nominal fee he could run a hosepipe from one of the milk churns into his battery operated teasmaid. When her business was slack Madame Mysterylingo nipped into the back of Pringle's taxi and read the balls of people's feet. Further up the rank a potter's wheel was going full belt in the back of a B.M.W. while another London-type cab featured a priest who was hearing confessions through the grille. "It's the brother home on holidays from the missions in Tanzania," explained the driver. "He's sort of keeping his hand in." Business is so good at the rank that none of the drivers want to take people anywhere. You can always use the DART but you have to supply your own bucket.

Please Love And Cherish Your Bus Inspector

I think that one of them must have frightened me when I was very small. Maybe he leaned over my pram and bit a lump out of my lollipop. I'm not really sure. A lot of people seem to feel the same way. Whenever I see one I get the same trembly feeling as when the bishop walked into the church with a headful of hard questions and you sat there in your confirmation suit repeating over and over in your head, "God made the world and St. Patrick came to Ireland in 432". Yet bus inspectors don't ask you to name all the cleaners on the night shift in Donnybrook Garage or who invented the ticket machine.

I'm sure that they're really very nice men who don't want to see a bus full of panic stricken passengers rooting in their pockets and turning their handbags inside out as soon as they climb aboard. A woman sitting near me said, "Oh Mammy" and blessed herself yesterday when an inspector got on at Fairview. She told me later that she works as a senior systems analyst in a huge multi-national company. There is something very seriously wrong when a person such as this says, "Oh Mammy".

I'm not suggesting that bus inspectors leap aboard shouting "I come from haunts of coot and hern" or chanting a hearty "Ho ho ho". It would be nice though if they said something like "Hello — I'm Kevin and I won't be cross with you if at this very moment your ticket is a soggy chewed-up lump. I won't even give out to you if you hand it to me in an infinite number of tiny confetti fragments."

Then he could warmly embrace the driver and join him in the duet from "The Pearl Fishers". I wouldn't feel quite so threatened then. I wouldn't feel impelled to sit there with my ticket held obediently up in the air and a "what a good little boy am I" sort of look on my face. Dublin Bus can do much to demystify their ticket checkers. A nice series of advertisements where he goes home at night and takes off his cap and says sadly to his wife ... "Why do people turn their handbags inside out when they see me coming: What is it about me that sends conductors hurtling upstairs if I even look sideways at their bus?"

Then she can embrace him and whisper: "Darling — you can banish me from a bus anytime into a raging blizzard and I'll still love you". His children can come romping in from the garden piping "Daddy, Daddy — check our tickets and make us pay the fare again ... we'll still love you because you tuck us in at night". Then his ageing father, who lives in the same house, can stand at the bottom of the stairs ringing an imaginary bell while his waybill is checked. The inspector can whisper lovingly, "God, but you're very good at the hard sums," while the old man murmurs, "More power to the crease in your uniformed trousers". Then the whole family can wander out into the garden to plant some more Lily of the Valley.

If he'd let us try on his cap when we were very small there wouldn't be half as many soggy tickets.

How Do You Get A Job Making Those Announcements?

I HAVEN'T got a clue what they're talking about. I don't even know which language they use. There I was in Heuston Station waiting to catch the train to Waterford. An announcement came over the loudspeaker: "Bras noodle nordle wick hung horgraden crumbled hopsididdle for Waterford." I didn't know what to think. When somebody announces a thing like that about your train you don't even know whether or not to panic. So I asked a man on the bench beside me. "What did she say about Waterford?" He said that he wasn't too sure but he thought it was something about noodle nordles and a crumpled hopsididdle.

I asked him did he know what a crumpled hopsididdle was and he said that he'd got problems of his own. "I'm waiting to go to Galway," he said. "And she announced five minutes ago that all passengers to Galway are to mogger wiggle rumscang on Platform Two immediately. How in the name of God do you do a thing like that?" I was afraid to even attempt a translation in case I made matters worse. He told me that bad and all as things might be, we were still better off than his cousin. "My cousin was on this station last year. He'd just arrived off the Wexford train when the woman announced that he was to vinglew crarn mogwerth in the station master's office as soon as possible. The poor man wasn't the better of it for a month." This is all very well when you're on your holidays in Bulgaria. You don't mind too much when a station announcement tells you

something like that. You half expect it. The fact that the Bulgarians can't understand it either is neither here nor there. But it's a bit much to be asked to vingle cram mogwerth in your own country. Then the flappers on the station indicator board start to whizz around and take you from Tralee to Dublin in five seconds.
Nobody is too sure how you get a job making these announcements. A man I know swears that you have to recite nursery rhymes in Serbo-Croat at halfspeed until the interview board pleads for mercy.
Then you sit in an echo chamber and read the ingredients for a marinated onion souffle through a six-foot-long Wavin pipe. You pause every thirty seconds to say: "This does not apply to passengers for Sligo." If selected for training you're expected to study a tape of the Pope's speech in the Phoenix Park and memorise the speeded-up version of Placido Domingo singing 'The Rocky Road To Dublin'. Then you are entrusted with the railway station announcer's secret. Nobody else knows that Lucky's speech in "Waiting for Godot" is a verbatim transcript of every announcement made on Heuston Station in the Summer of 1951.
You wouldn't be up to Samuel Beckett.

Pat Ingoldsby's Cure For Fear Of Flying

Some airlines have already tried it. Certain window seats in the aircraft are reserved for people who are terrified of flying.
Before take-off they have exactly the same view as the other passengers. But as soon as the plane moves off

down the runway, the picture changes dramatically. They are looking out at a herd of Jersey cows grazing peacefully in a meadow. Right beside the window.
To heighten the illusion, one of the cows ambles over and peers in at you. Stereophonic mooing sounds on your headphones while the hostess shouts "G'wan—hup! hup!" Her timing is impeccable because she has undergone an intensive study both of the film and animal husbandry.
On a signal from her, the captain puts on a smock and wanders back from the flight-deck clanking a bucket "Ar . . . ar," he announces. "It be time to go outside and milk the herd in the Long Meadow."
He only says this to selected passengers who are seated at the special windows. This is most important.
During the early stages of the experiment, an airline captain announced to an elderly couple that he was going outside to spancil a heifer. The plane was six miles above the Atlantic. They held hands and sang hymns for the remainder of the flight.
When it operates according to plan, the scheme is most effective. As soon as the captain has disappeared from view with his bucket, the selected passengers see him in a field outside seated on a three-legged stool. When he reappears the bucket is filled with fresh milk which is then used for the coffee
Timing is of the essence. Several passengers were gravely concerned at seeing the captain clanking his bucket in the aisle while simultaneously being chased across the field by a bullock.

Aer Lingus have been using the Supertrain illusion to good affect. Selected passengers get the impression from their windows that they are rail travelling from Dublin to Cork. Stations and bridges shoot past. Communication cords are fitted above their seats. They are not however, connected to the flight-deck.
It is absolutely necessary to keep these passengers strictly apart from the others. An Israeli couple were gazing down on the Austrian Alps when a wild-eyed Mayo man told them he should have got off three miles back at Mallow.
When they said they were staying on till Rome he said wasn't it cat altogether and went looking for the guard's van. Hostesses are mildly confused by the experiments. "When you look out the window," one of them said, "it's either Limerick Junction, Kennedy International or a herd of Charolais — we don't know where we are." They must learn to keep things like this to themselves.

Make One Sudden Move And Your Gone

"Don't anybody put your hand down."
The woman's voice rang out loud and clear as she entered the carriage. Her dog trotted along beside her. "It's his first time on a train so keep your hands in — he snaps things off when he's upset."
We sat there frozen. Nobody as much as twitched a moving part. The woman moved slowly along the aisle explaining to us about the crucial "do's and don'ts" as she passed between us.

"Hector is very protective towards me," she said. "If anybody looks like they're going to grab me he goes into action."

It seemed like a reasonable enough arrangement. Nobody was to grab at her between Heuston and Galway. In return for our restraint, Hector wouldn't bite anything off.

The woman's dog settled down quite happily on his blanket. "The most dangerous time will come when the train starts," she explained to the man sitting opposite her. "Once Hector gets through that trauma we should be alright." The man retreated into a private trauma of his very own. He lit a cigarette with slow careful movements. "That's not such a bad day," he croaked. The woman's reply merely compounded his trauma. "We'll know in a couple of minutes," she said.

Hector went into a deep sleep during which he released irregular yapping noises. "He has recurring dreams about his father," she said. "He was run over by a bread-van." Without any warning she began to sing 'There's a pawn-shop on the corner in Pittsburgh Pennsylvania' and Hector's sleep-yapping stopped. "He likes Guy Mitchell," she said.

A man in a white shirt arrived trundling his coffee trolley along the aisle. "For God's sake don't stop or he'll think you're going to attack me," warned the woman. It was too late. Hector woke, took one look at the trolley and decided that here at last was the enemy. He snarled a series of ultimatums and exploded into a frenzy of final warnings.

"Pet it," said the woman.

"I beg your pardon," said the man.
"Pet your coffee trolley and I'll pet it too. Hector thinks it's another dog."
Together they stroked the trolley and said, "There's a good boy". The woman told it to *sit* and started to sing. She serenaded it with 'She Wears Red Feathers and a Hula Hula Skirt' until Hector went back into a deep sleep. "Now," she said, "I'll have a cup of tea please — two sugars".
We reached Galway without further incident. I think it's because nobody in the carriage made any sudden movements and the woman knew lots of Guy Mitchell songs. It's amazing how long a train journey can be when you're afraid to move.

Into The West

God knows I did my best for him. I used to roar at the top of my voice "Don't go into town Tonto! They'll only whack you over the head again, and then where will you be?" They were always at it ... belting the poor guy with iron bars, pick-axe handles and bottles. It's a mystery to me how he was able to put one foot in front of the other.
It was all very well for The Lone Ranger. There he was preaching about making the West a fit place for ladies in flowery bonnets, and quite right too. But in the next breath he'd be saying: "You go into town Tonto and see what you can find out." I prayed that just once he would

respond: "Blow it out your arse Kemo Sabay — I'm off to the reservation for a good fertility dance."
The Lone Ranger always failed to give him clear instructions. He never said: "Go into town and check out the price of flowery bonnets," or "See if you can find me a really good reference book on Bible History." This is the reason why the poor befuddled Indian spent the best years of his life hiding in doorways and peeping in through windows. He was trying to find something out even though he hadn't got the faintest idea what the moralist in the mask wanted to know.
I swear to God there was even special BELTING TONTO OVER THE HEAD background music. You could hear it coming a mile off. Oh shit here comes the music ... THUD! They never shot Tonto. I'll give them that much. Perhaps they enjoyed his periodic visits to town so much that the thought never crossed their minds. It was possibly the high spot of their week. "What'll we do today guys? Oh ... hang on ... Tonto's coming to town this afternoon to see what he can find out ... Yeehaw!" One particular week I nearly died. It was fierce. There was Tonto with his ear pressed up against someone's back door having a listen, and by God did he choose the wrong door. All of a sudden he was surrounded by a really mean gang of desperadoes with black stubbly chins, scuffy hats and decidedly low standards, and they were all yelling, "String the redskin up!" God, I thought that was a bit extreme. It wasn't as if he was having a furtive peep at ladies besporting themselves in their flowery bonnets. He was merely

pressing his ear up against a door as was his wont, and by jiminy you don't string people up for that.

I was in the sitting room yelling "Quick ... Quick ... they're lynching Tonto!" Father came charging in from the back garden, my mother came hurtling down the stairs two steps at a time and my sister was sent up the road to tell my brothers to hurry up or they'd miss it. "You're sure they're not just whacking him over the head again?" my brothers demanded, and my sister swore blind that they had a rope and everything.

You should have seen him. Sitting there proud and erect on his piebald pony with a rope around his neck and sort of forgiveness in his eyes. He knew it was what Kemo Sabay would have wished. My sister was crying. My granny was shouting, "Leave him alone you thundering shower of bullies!"

It was an amazing shot — I'll give him that much. I mean — how many people do you know who can hurtle down a street at full gallop roaring 'HI HO SILVER' at the top of his voice and pierce a rope with one bullet? Fair enough, he might go on a bit about flowery bonnets, upright ranchers and silver bullets, but he sure as hell got Tonto out of that one.

As they thundered out of town side by side Tonto turned to his masked companion and delivered the truly remarkable line: "That was plenty bad Kemo Sabay." Of course it was plenty bad, Tonto. And it will be plenty worse in the future if you don't wise up and tell that masked pillock to do his own snoopy work. Listen man ... head off to the reservation for one of those truly energising fertility dances. God knows you've earned it.

Daniel O'Donnell and The Ball Of Wool

Will someone please tell me how they do it? I've seen it loads of times, and it is wrecking my head. You know the television ad where the lovely gentle white-haired lady is knitting a tea-cosy or something, and Daniel O'Donnell is doing a gig in her sitting room. All of a sudden the ball of wool rolls off her lap and hits the floor. How do they do that? How do they get it to roll exactly on cue?

The lady certainly doesn't do a cheaty thing like waggling her legs because I've put my head right up against the screen and checked her out. You can take my word for it - there's nothin' shaking but the leaves on the trees. Anyway, Daniel would never become professionally involved with a cheaty waggle. No sir.

Then I thought ... hang on a second ... supposing that the gentle lady is concealing a little automatic spring about her person ... a little spring with a built-in time switch. It performs a sudden secret 'boing', and hey ho here we go — the ball of wool is rolling. I rushed around to my Aunty Annie and borrowed the huge magnifying glass which she uses to locate fleas in her duffle coat. Then I asked my sister to video the ad for me, and I watched it over and over again through the magnifying glass, and I froze the frame and everything. If there are any hidden little boings going on in there, I sure as hell can't find them.

Remote control! Aha! You know that guy ... the kindly well-meaning Professor Horst MacHenry who is always inventing things for the good of mankind because that is how he is. He cares. But his inventions are forever falling into the wrong hands and his daughter gets kidnapped and tied to railway tracks. Well for once I feel pretty confident that Horst had got nothing to do with this one. I believe that he has learned his lesson. My god — the poor man invented a device for keeping senior citizens' boiled eggs warm in igloos, and you remember as well as I do what happened. It was stolen and used to liquidise Blue Whales. No — the professor has had it up to here, thank you very much.

They may have approached him. They probably did. "Eh Horst ... we're doing this TV thing .. right up your street really ... we need a special ball of wool capable of leaping off an old lady's lap and seeking out Daniel O'Donnell."

You'd never walk old Horst into an assignment like that. Not any more. For one thing his daughter is browned off being kidnapped. The poor girl hasn't slept in her own bed two nights running for over a year. And secondly, Horst realises that a heat-seeking ball of wool in the wrong hands could change the whole face of wage negotiations as we know it. No bloody fear.

I give up. If you know how they do it please tell me. You will not find me ungrateful. I can recite Saint Augustine's Confessions for you in Latin at the bus stop of your choice. You can borrow my little silver hammer if you've got some toffee which you need to smash in a hurry. That's about it really.

I borrowed a Daniel O'Donnell tape and a ball of wool, and sat there with it on my lap for three bloody hours, but nothing happened. I was tempted to waggle ... I have to be honest, I really was. That's original sin for you. But I didn't. Neither would Horst. No sir.

How Granny Fixed Dixie Dean

There is nothing like ten years on the road doing children's gigs for finely honing your survival techniques. Nothing you have ever learned in assertion books can prepare you for the sight of 5,000 wildly excited children packed into the Dome in Tralee during Rose Week. A sight like that can make all the hair on your body suddenly go white ... under your arms and everywhere. I'll show you the photographs if you don't believe me. God, when I think of it ... standing in the wings with a roast chicken on my head ... a roast chicken with a blue telephone perched on top. 5,000 frenzied children chanting "We want Pat's Hat ... We want Pat's Hat" and me thinking "It's not my hat I'm worried about". Manic visions of teddy bears with their stuffing pulled out ... dolls with their arms and legs missing ... Christians being hunted up the walls of amphitheatres by hungry lions who didn't believe in the infallibility of the Pope.

My brain was telling my legs to work and my legs were saying "Blow it out your nozzle ... we're on the first bus out of here." The sound of 5,000 creche-wreckers chanting my name, whipped the batteries out of my legs and rampaged through my vocabulary with a Tipp-Ex brush. I froze backstage with empty legs and all my words missing and I prayed to my granny. My favourite one. The granny who died in Dublin, lived in Chester and put the fear of God into Dixie Dean. She truly did. Dixie Dean was a soccer legend and my granny took him right to the edge of the precipice and dangled him over with her finger and thumb.

When I was a kid I wrote to him for his autograph and he never wrote back. So I sent a letter to my granny. Poor Dixie didn't know what was coming. *Cry havoc. Let loose the dogs of war.* I'm not sure what she said to him when she rampaged into his Chester pub — the lovely historic tavern with all his English international caps on display in glass cases. I'm not sure if she got a firm grip on him, hoisted him off the floor and stood him on his own counter. I sincerely hope that she didn't. You don't do that to soccer legends. Whatever indignities she inflicted on him I received an astonishing letter from the most famous centre forward in soccer history pleading with me to forgive him. Rock on granny wherever you are. Up Chester.

I did one show in a farmyard in Cappaghwhite during a Macra na Feirme Field Night. It was mind-blowing. There was a 'Guess the Number of Holes in the String Vest' competition. I personally won the 'Throw Three Bristly Brushes into a Milk Churn' contest. I was utterly astonished by my victory and so were the farmers who had been practising behind their barns all winter. It wasn't one bit fair and I was the first to admit it. I had never thrown a bristly brush at a milk churn in my life before. Not even in anger. So I gave the trophy back and they didn't insert me into a combine harvester. It was a reasonable exchange.

I did one show on the back of a lorry during a torrential downpour in the main square at Michelstown. Lashing rain, live microphones and me a fingertip touch away from vaporising myself into a fizzling hiss of human steam. Every time the canvas canopy bulged down and tried to absorb me into its huge splodge, one of the committee lunged up into it with the blunt end of a sweeping brush and a silver sheet of uisce swooshed down in front of the stage. The audience huddled in their cars with the windscreen wipers swaying. They beeped their horns instead of applauding. My head was wrecked for a month.

I did one show inside a container on the back of a lorry in a sun-scorched field. The sound system was a portable radio in my left hand and a microphone in my right. The children were sent in to me in batches of 50. I was right down the far end in semi-darkness. When I entered the container the field outside was thronged with lively holiday people. When I was led from it very slowly three hours later, they had all become translucent giraffes with hockey-stick legs and mandarin oranges where their heads should be. I am not the better of it yet. Speak softly to me if you will.

Off The Rails

Some people prefer to sit at the back of a plane because of the theory put forward by Tommy Cooper that aircraft do not reverse into mountains. And quite right too. I choose not to sit anywhere near the back of an Iarnrod Eireann Inter-City train because I love turkey sandwiches with chutney. Believe me you've got no chance at the back. You can forget the ham and tuna as well. By the time the trolley reaches you there's nothing left except boiling water and the stuff that nobody else wants — pimple sandwiches and flu-virus crisps and you're bloody lucky to get them.

I don't give out to the trolley person because it certainly isn't her fault. When all seemed lost she produced a tuna sandwich without a trace of pimple and God forgive me, I still wanted to know what was wrong with it. As far as I'm concerned if a single tuna sandwich traverses the whole length of an InterCity train without anybody making a half-decent offer for it, the first thing I'm going to do is scrutinise the wrapper for telltale words like toenails, fainting fits or The Siege of Limerick.

I was trudging along the train in the Cork direction to buy a can of Finches Orange when I caught up with the trolley on its return journey to the dining car. I was amazed to still see it because I had urged the trolley person: "Your mission if you choose to accept it is to arrive in Mallow before the train does." — and I truly thought she had taken up the challenge.

When you come upon the trolley in mid-carriage there is simply no way past. You join the tailback of six or seven people and you inch along at stop/start pace and you are well and truly snookered. This is the reason why Butch Cassidy and Sundance and the other guys from Hole in the Wall used to half-run, half-leap along the roof. They wanted a can of Finches, and who can blame them? I call upon the Spiritual Directors of Iarnrod Eireann to instigate an inspiring new religion known henceforth as FOLLOWERS OF THE TROLLEY. It will give us something enriching to do, and more importantly it will keep us all off the roof. *Go bhoire Dia orainn* — if you get a belt of a low bridge all the compensation in the world wouldn't get you right.

You know the way there are little red hammers inside glass boxes on the trains. I think they're lovely. I especially like the way you have to borrow a high-heeled shoe to get the hammer out. I know a man who met his wife that way and God bless the pair of them. I would like to see additional little boxes shaped like cathedral windows. There can be stained glass in them and everything. Each box shall contain one of those nice roundy incense burners on a silver chain. No other country in the world has thought of this so bah jeery bah!

When you're stuck behind the trolley you smash the glass with a loud shout of 'HOPSIDIDDLE!' Then you all parade along behind the trolley singing hymns, releasing doves, lashing out the incense and giving thanks for turkey, tuna and chutney.

I am sort of willing to be Acting Head of FOLLOWERS OF THE TROLLEY providing they don't go starting religious wars or expect me to live on top of a mountain in a converted railway carriage. I tell you what I'd really love to do. I'd love to work on one of those trolleys for a week or so and change all the 'Best Before' dates on the sandwiches. Change them to things like 'Best before Athenry' ... 'Best before Thurles'. That should put a tad more interest into it.

Oh — if you'd like to witness something truly astonishing, hide in the bushes at the side of the railway tracks. Wait until about four in the morning. This is the time when some huge big metal pylons out in the fields begin to swing their arms and twirl their electric wires round and round and chant: "All in together girls, never mind the weather girls, get your hats, get your coats, get your umbrellas girls" and all the cows have the time of their lives skipping until the sun comes up. Oh yes they do!!!

This Free Travel Can Ruin Your Granny

You can't call your granny your own anymore. This is the clear message being received by Iarnrod Eireann. "Give our kiddies back their Nana" is the demand being made by furious parents.

More and more wild-eyed grannies are careering around the country with the free-travel and an ever-growing number of children are suffering from severe 'Nana Loss'. Concerned parents are picketing Iarnrod Eireann headquarters with placards which read 'Hands off our Nanas'.

There was no problem at first with the free-travel. Grannies went into town on the bus and said their Nana-prayers in the Pro-Cathedral. Then they came straight home again.

Granny Hegarty was the first to venture outside of the Dublin area. She went to 12 o'clock Mass in the Pro and wasn't seen again for six days. The old lady went completely out of control and was spotted by indepen-

dent witnesses in Cork, Galway, Sligo and Donegal in the space of 48 hours.
"Don't stop me now, man," she said to a railway porter on Heuston Station. "I gotta groove on down to Cork before the sweet shops close." The woman was clearly in the grip of what rock musicians call road fever.
Iarnrod Eireann are concerned about chronic granny congestion at Mallow and Limerick Junction. On any given day, hundreds of nanas with nostrils flared and pupils dilated are waiting for connecting trains to places as far apart as Tralee and Bandon.
Some of them are boogie-ing up and down the platform with arms linked, chanting: "Here we go, here we go, here we go" and swopping the addresses of sweet shops which offer the best value in fizz bags and Liqourish Pipes.
"They are not exactly intimidating our other passengers at the moment," said an Iarnrod spokesperson. "But somebody is going to get trampled in the rush whenever a train pulls in."
Some grannies are sleeping rough on railway stations. "My little girl was devastated when we were bringing her to the beach in Malahide last summer," sobbed one distraught mother. "Her nana had gone out to collect her pension and was missing for a month. We told Natalie that she was down in Adam and Eve's praying for good bingo numbers. The poor little child couldn't believe her eyes when we got to Connolly Station and there was her granny curled up sound asleep in her favourite rug under a bench with a beatific glow on her

face. She was clutching the free pass in one hand and a half-eaten bag of fizz in the other."

Behavioural Psychologists are grappling with a three-fold problem. Nanas who are out of their heads on road fever, children suffering from acute Granny-Deprivation and reports that some of the old ladies are mainlining on neat fizz.

If we give them free flights, we might never see them again.

The Building Societies Shall Not Have Them

The bank manager had just given his staff a pep talk. "The building societies are after our customers," he said. "Posters and radio ads everywhere ... you've all heard them ... nothing is too much trouble ... we'll stand on our heads for you ... we'll stay open at lunchtime ... in fact it breaks our hearts to go home at all ... we love you and your children and your goldfish and your budgie."

The bank staff nodded. "It's up to each and everyone of you to radiate warmth and love and make our customers feel that we'd even sew their missing buttons back on for them if we had a needle and thread. The building societies shall not have them." One by one his staff took deep breaths and returned to their posts.

An hour later, Nigel Thwisk walked into the bank with a large plastic bag over his shoulder. "Could I have a pound's worth of penny pieces?" he asked the cashier. "I'm just off to the laundrette and I need change for the driers." The cashier's eyes softened. She smiled lovingly.

"I'll take it home and do it for you," she offered. "And my mother will be happy to iron your shirts."

Nigel smiled uncertainly. The thought of anybody's mother setting eyes on his red and white candystriped thingimajigs filled him with advanced trembles. "Ah no, thanks," he stammered. "I have to do it myself as part of my assertion and self-development therapy."

But the cashier was mainlining on love now and there was no stopping her. "I tell you what we'll do," she said. "We'll credit-transfer the bag down to the laundrette for you."

Before Nigel knew what was happening he was filling up a bank-giro slip and his bag of washing had been absorbed into the system.

Nigel was down-town an hour later when he realised he needed a clean shirt for that very evening. He raced into the bank's head office and filled out a withdrawal docket. "Can I have my cleanest dirty shirt please?" he asked the cashier. "I lodged the lot in your Clontarf branch."

The cashier checked his computer. "I'm sorry, but it hasn't shown up yet." Fortunately for Nigel the head-office staff had just had a pep talk as well.

"If you step in behind that potted palm tree," murmured the cashier. "I'll be out to you in a second." Not only that but the other male cashiers filtered out too and took Nigel Thwisk's chest measurements. Then they whipped off their shirts and in a matter of seconds the job was right. Nigel had a crisp white shirt and the cashiers whispered happily to each other — "The building societies shall not have them."

The fact that Nigel's bag of washing was inadvertently credited to a retired pork butcher's savings account is neither here nor there. These things happen. When the day comes that you can get a clean pair of socks out of a Pass machine, the banks will never look back.

Time-waster Queues

I'd love to know the question. I'd love to know the question which some people ask when they reach the top of the queue in the GPO. They lean forward and ask it in a whisper and the person behind the counter gets up and goes away somewhere. They get up and they go away and they don't come back for ages. Sometimes they don't come back at all. Where do they go? What do they do when they get there? I'd love to know.
Anybody can slow down a queue in the GPO. It's as easy as trying to send a pair of hedgehogs surface-mail to Tanzania. It's as easy as trying to register a sheep's pancreas. Anybody can do that. But the question. That is the real clincher. Not just any question. No sir. I'm talking about THE QUESTION ... the one which causes stamp counter officials to abandon their posts and take refuge in the secret room and remain there in prayer and meditation for ages. That's the one I'm after. God knows I've tried. I've tried asking: "How many postmen called Nigel who live west of the Galtee Mountains thrust their left leg into their trousers first?" I've tried asking: "How do you get the silvery balloons down again when they float up to the ceiling?" But so far I've failed to crack it.

There used to be a system of buttons on Dublin docks. Perhaps there still is. The button is passed down from father to son. It is revered. It is treasured. Something similar happens with taxi plates. Perhaps it is the same sort of thing with the question. When a father is about to expire he beckons his son forward to the edge of the bed and he whispers: "My son — what I am about to divulge to you is a secret of mind-trembling power ... I am about to impart to you the mystical question which is capable of paralysing a stamp queue for all eternity ... and the question is ..."

But what is it? Do you know? Did your Da whisper it to you? If so, will you whisper it to me if I give you a signed copy of my new poetry book? What? OK then ... two copies.

It's not quite so bad on Heuston Station but you do get people who are quite incapable of simply handing over their money, buying a ticket and that is that. I call upon Iarnrod Eireann to open up a special window with a sign over the top - "THIS WINDOW IS RESERVED FOR THE MALCONTENTS WHO FEEL THE NEED TO COMPLICATE MATTERS WITH DOCKETS, VOUCHERS, WARRANTS, BLOCK BOOKINGS AND PINK FORMS WITH COMPLETE HURLING TEAMS ON THEM." Give these people a window all to themselves and let them have the time of their lives holding one another up so that they miss their trains. Leave the rest of us in peace. All we want is our tickets and nothing else.

British Superloos

I couldn't believe my ears.
"It'll cost you 10p to come in here." That's what the woman in the ticket office told me. My goodness, I thought. That is two shillings in old money. I remember the time when you could buy yourself six choc ices for that.
And here I am being asked for an investment of 10p to go into a Superloo on Inverness Railway station to do one single solitary wee wee. Six HB choc ices. One wee wee. How the once mighty pound has fallen.
I paid my 10p because I was bursting. When I was finished I washed my neck and face as well, brushed my boots up against the back of my jeans, irrigated the spaces between my teeth with a match stick and changed the battery in my hearing aid. I was determined to get my money's worth. Then I went back to the urinal and did another tiny little subsidiary wee wee worth about 1½p.
Outside on the platform I worked out a hurried sum on the back of an envelope. Based on an average daily output of six wee wees during my 52 years on this earth, I estimated that at British Rail piddling rates that lot would have cost me £11,388.00. I went straight back to the ticket office and I told the woman. In fact it should be more because I have omitted to include Leap Years in that figure.
She said that if it would make me any happier I was welcome to have one on the house and throw in one of my number twos for good measure, but I don't think

she was being very sincere because she was smiling like one of those women who used to knit bolero jackets while watching French aristocrats' heads bouncing into wicker baskets.

There was worse to follow. Two days later I was waiting for a train on Edinburgh Station. I was knotting my legs together. Little beads of perspiration were glistening on my forehead. Hold on a little longer, I was telling myself. Any minute now you'll be on the train and then you can do it for nothing. The water pressure was mounting. Bright silver spots were jiggling up and down in front of my eyes. I was about to explode. It was widdle or bust.

"You'll have to put another 20p in there," said the man in the ticket office. "It's 30p." Good God — that's another 12 choc ices in old money. I was in no shape to argue, so I whammed in the extra money and hurtled inside. When I was finished I changed my socks, cleared out both ears with a cotton bud, trimmed my moustache, stuck a can of deodorant up my jumper and sprayed my stomach, went into a cubicle and sat down for twenty minutes even though I didn't want to do anything, and then flushed away all the toilet paper in the place. 30 pence worth is right.

Euston Station in London is different again. There you can choose between two different wee wee emporiums. Business men in expensive suits delight in paying 30 pence. This entitles you to release an executive class, decisive, management-structured piddle in the Super-Duper, Rarefied, Upwardly Exclusive Flusherama. Only people who know their place would aspire to widdling in there. All others either pay 20 pence further down the platform or vault over the turnstiles when nobody is looking. I thought, to hell with it. This is my last day in Britain. Let's do the thing in style. Let's try a corporate tinkle.

This time there were no turnstiles. Instead I was welcomed by a uniformed attendant who gave me my pink ticket and a white serviette.

Good heavens, I thought, they must be serving complimentary meals in here as well. But they weren't. The whole thing was a swindle. There was no classical music or heated seats or chrome handles or anything. Your bottom wasn't pampered by perfumed jets of air or billowing clouds of exotic talcum powder. I honestly expected dusky men in coloured silken Aladdin trousers and shoes with curly bits at the front to be carrying trays full of free electric toothbrushes and tiny golden scissors for trimming the hairs which sometimes sprout out of your nose. Superloo my arse. I've found more stimulation on Connolly Station when the lock is broken and the door jams and you can't get out again and someone has to go and get a porter. Erin go brath! Five lighters for a pound!

Penile Relaxation

My penis is bad tempered and grumpy and irritable and I don't really blame it. I got this relaxation tape to calm my body down because I'm getting all tense and uptight and everything.

Back home I lay on my floor with my head on the beanbag and listened to my relaxation tape. It was brilliant as far as it went. The husky voice began at the top of my head and worked its way down, giving me lovely messages of peace and calm. My neck and shoulders never felt so good. Then on down over my chest and my stomach with tranquil ease. I felt great.

Then it happened. The husky voice skipped on down to my legs in one leap. It completely ignored my penis. From my tummy to my legs as if my poor hypertensive willy wasn't there at all. "Hey!" I said to the tape. "You've missed one of my bits. Can we go back up to my stomach and start again?" I was wasting my bloody time because tapes can't hear you. So I rewound it to the tummy part and played it again. The same thing happened. Where is the sense in having a tape like that?

The first time I sensed trouble after that was when I opened my zip and my penis bit a lump out of my finger. I swear. I was freaked. My thoughts were panic-stricken. "Do I need an immediate tetanus shot or what? Perhaps I'll die in the next five minutes from rabies or something." So I phoned a hospital outpatients and said very urgently — "My penis has just bitten me — should I rush straight in for oxygen or will I lie down in a darkened room? Please advise me."

Reproductive organs don't usually go around biting lumps out of their owners. Not without provocation anyway. So I rang off and put butter on my finger. Actually it was 94 pence Vitalite because I can't afford butter at the moment.

The next time I sensed trouble was when I was sitting beside a woman on the bus. Everything was grand. She was looking out the window and I was reading my book. Without warning my penis gave a grumpy growl. I was mortified. Then it began to snarl like a little yappy dog. Granted, the sound was a bit muffled because it was coming from inside my jeans but the woman heard it all the same. "Have you got a dog under the seat or what?" she asked.

"Not quite," I replied. "I've got this rare miniature breed of dog in my pocket and he's not feeling the best because I didn't bring him for walkies this morning." Things got steadily worse after that because the woman said, "Oh I see. How fascinating. I'm actually a breeder myself. Eh — what type is it?" Before I knew where I was I heard myself saying, "It's an Andalusian Yapping Shepherd which lives in people's pockets. There are only three of them in the entire world. The other two live in a pair of trousers in Cairo." I really shouldn't have told her that. The bloody woman was intrigued. "I ... I wonder could I see it?" she enquired .

"Daylight gives them visions," I explained. "If I take him out of my pocket suddenly there's no knowing what he will do. If you like you can whisper: 'Who's a pretty boy then?' Andalusian Yapping Shepherds love that." She said very briskly: "Sit!" I'm not quite sure why she said that but she said it anyway. All of a sudden the grumpy growling stopped. It was quite remarkable. My jeans fell silent and I said to her: "Well fair play to you anyway."

"Thank you," she said demurely.

"You're welcome," I replied. Isn't life wonderful all the same. If you put a tune to that you could sing it. Yippeee!

The Good Old Days

I wish that I'd been around in The Good Old Days. My grandmother used to tell me all about them. It was one hell of a time to be alive. "Me and your grandad would go into town in a taxi and have a five-course meal in the Gresham with a bottle of champagne in a bucket, and when we came out we still had change from a pound. So we'd go on to the Olympia Theatre and pay for a private box all to ourselves, eat lashings of expensive hand-made chocolates and have another bottle in a bucket during the interval. When we came out I'd say to grandad: 'How's the money holding up there Kevin?' and he'd say to me: 'Feck it anyway Nancy... we've still got change from a pound... what'll we do now?' You couldn't even give it away because Dublin was full of couples wandering around the place counting their money and saying to one another, 'Well blast it, Sheila — that Mediterranean cruise was a waste of time... we've still got change from a pound — you're gettin' another fur coat whether you want it or not and that's final."' In them days everybody had a bit of respect. My grandad said that you'd get a flying kick in the ribs from a Christian Brother who'd be wearing a hefty pair of metal-tipped boots. "But you didn't mind a bit because it was teaching you respect," he said. "Sometimes the teacher would lift you up out of your seat and your ear came off and the teacher ate it, but you never complained because in them days your ear grew again inside a week. Everyone was going around the place lifting their hats to ladies and saluting priests and putting their jackets down over puddles and offering one another change from a pound and growing new ears by the week. And if you saw a guard you'd salute him and say: 'More power to your truncheon', because they had truncheons in them days and if you got a belt over the head with one you didn't mind a bit because you knew it was for your own good... in fact you even whipped off your hat so he could get a really decent whack at you..."

The key was always in the door. Before my grandparents went to bed at night they piled up all granny's jewelry in the hall. Beside it they placed grandad's pocket watch and lots of little bags filled with change from pounds. Then they knelt down and thanked God for all the kicks in the ribs and whacks over the head with truncheons. Next morning when they came downstairs they discovered that somebody had polished all the jewelry during the night, wound the watch and neatly arranged the money into little orderly stacks of shillings and florins and half-crowns. Sometimes complete strangers had even let themselves into the house and wall-papered the sitting room. That's the sort of thing you did in The Good Old Days when you couldn't sleep. You let yourself into other people's houses and sewed missing buttons onto their trousers or swept their chimney while they were sleeping. God as my witness, there'd be some nights when nobody'd be in their own house at all.

And they were happy. Granny said you'd be roaring laughing if you fell under a tram or somebody flung you bodily off the top of Nelson's Pillar. You'd be laughing all the way down because you knew that somebody somewhere was worse off than yourself. In fact they were the last words that grandad spoke before he sank for the third time in a vat of swampy porridge. "Not to worry Nancy," he said, "Isn't somebody somewhere worse off?' He was absolutely right. Even as he spoke, Mr Hanratty next door was being sucked up the chimney feet first by an imploding Zeppelin which had crash-landed on his roof. He didn't mind a bit either "Yippee!" The last word he shouted. You'd have to.

Poems In The Pond

My first ever television appearance as a poet nearly killed me. I wanted the whole thing to be authentic and true to the central theme of the piece which was titled 'This Poem Solemnly Asserts The Sacred Right Of Each And Every Irish Duck To Complete Freedom Of Quacks Whenever Each And Every Irish Duck Feels So Inclined'.

And quite right too.

That was why I asked the producer if he could fill the studio with real live ducks who could perform synchronised waddles and unified quacks while I stood on top of a waterbarrel and recited my poem to them. I honestly thought it was a great idea.

The first production meeting decided that they didn't want duck shite all over Studio One. The second meeting recalled that some weeks ago a temperamental swan had almost pecked somebody's eyes out in Studio Two. The third meeting clinched it. "Why don't we go to where the ducks are?" suggested a production assistant. Everyone said "Absolutely" and "Excellent".
It wasn't anybody's fault that our first attempt in St. Stephen's Green was a shambles. We simply underestimated the ducks. I stood at the edge of the pond and recited my poem with deep feeling, but they completely betrayed me. They huddled together on the far side and muttered uneasily amongst themselves: "Don't look now guys but there's some fuckwit over there waving his arms around and shouting rhyming stuff... keep your heads down and pretend you can't see him."
The producer was demanding ducks. The camera crew were firing lovely lumps of home-made brown bread into the water. A couple of bystanders were doing seductive mating calls and deep throated quacks, but the ducks were far from convinced. I felt like crying because I could see my first big television break falling apart. I was terrified that everyone was going to call it a day and pack up and go home and I'd never be asked to do anything again.
That is why I suggested taking off my shoes and socks, rolling up my jeans and wading in. The water was icy cold because we were filming in mid-winter. The bottom of the pond was all mucky and slippery and I was afraid that I'd go on my ear and drown myself. The ducks were now profoundly freaked. "Jesus guys — it's

getting worse... he's in the water." I realise it seems like the height of certifiable insanity now, but it made perfect sense at the time to wade ashore and suggest a pair of bathing togs because my jeans were soaked clean through. Someone legged it down to Grafton Street and came back with a really upmarket pair of stripey yokes. I didn't have a caravan with my name on the door or anything like that so I got changed in the bushes and all the time I was saying my poem over and over to myself because I was terrified of forgetting it. I was petrified with the cold.

It's incredible how quickly word spreads that someone in stripey bathing togs and a black hat is wandering around in the ornamental pond intimidating the ducks. A huge crowd gathered and they were all excited and shouting things and holding up children and everything. My nerves were in shreds. I was standing out in the middle of the pond saying my poem to myself over and over again while the camera crew were lining up their shots. Then the producer decided that there was still something missing.

"Shouldn't he be holding a gadget of some description? I mean, the poem is all about ducks being dequacked, so surely he should be pointing some sort of dequacking device at them." I was called ashore for a moment, given a camera tripod to hold and instructed to pretend that it was a digital duck dequacker. I am not making any of this up. You couldn't.

The last verse was the worst. Acting upon the producer's suggestion I took a deep breath and sank under the water. "Stay submerged for as long as you can while we get a shot of your hat floating away." The shock of it nearly killed me. I got £40, great artistic fulfillment and pleurisy.

Sound Advice

My sister said don't be ridiculous.
Cats don't eat hearing-aids. They much prefer things without hard batteries in them like mice or birds or other people's dinners.
That's all very well I said, but Chivers is licking her lips the way that cats do when they have just munched something AND she was playing with my hearing-aid AND now I can't find it anywhere.
For a week or so I heard the world in mono. Listening to sounds with one ear only. I rang the vet and he said no Pat, cats do not eat hearing-aids, but ostriches do. Then I remembered. Chivers had a distinctly ostrichey look on her face. I'd swear that she creeps out to golf courses at night and buries her head in bunkers.
I rang my sister. "Please pick Chivers up and hold her flat against a wall or a door or something. If she gives out a high-pitched sonic whistle we need search no further."
The test was inconclusive.
My sister's washing-machine says "Heinrich" over and over again while it is swishing the clothes around in water. Perhaps it is trying to tell her its name. I'm not sure really. It never says anything else. After doing a complete wash my sister was ironing a pillow case when it gave out a little gurgling sort of a whistle. She recognised the sound. It was the mating-call of the

waterlogged hearing-aid which wanted to make love to my left ear one more time before it became all rusty and drowned. A quick blast with a hot hairdryer and it was sonic-whistling again. All the gurgles were gone. Once again it was fully capable of disorientating bats and grievously confusing sheepdogs. I have since discovered something very exciting. If you also own a hearing-aid you might care to try it. Place it inside a pillow case and let it go through a complete cycle in a washing machine. Banish the gurgles with a hairdryer and put it back into your ear. I promise you the results will be astounding. I am now able to hear my commuter ticket going out of date at midnight on Saturdays. I hold it up against my ear and listen very closely and the poor ticket gives a piteous little whimper. The magnetic strip on the back releases a tiny melancholy sigh and that's it...

I now prefer to stay inside my house on Tuesdays until the binmen are gone. Believe me — the agonised shrieks and screams of the black plastic bags would vaporise your kidney stones. As the binmen approach I can clearly hear the bags whispering: "We're rightly bollixed now lads... quick... run for it!"

Unfortunately, they don't have any legs. That is the big problem about being a black plastic bag on bin morning. Suddenly you are whammed into the back of the lorry and those huge metal teeth come crushing down and I swear to you I would sooner listen to a million commuter tickets doing their whimpers than hear one bin bag going through the grinder. The language out of them would ruin your supper.

I no longer find it possible to relax on a barstool with a rock shandy unless I turn my hearing-aid off first. Initially I wasn't exactly sure of what I was picking up. It sounded like wave after wave of muted moans and groans and it was coming from the direction of the upside-down bottles of whiskey and vodka and gin behind the bar. Then I figured it out... of course... when I was a kid I used to stand on my head and all the blood would rush down and make me dizzy. It is exactly the same for the bottles. All the whiskey and gin and stuff presses down against their stoppers and gives them fierce headaches and visions. They live for the moment when the barman pushes a glass up under them and relieves a bit of the pressure. They heave little sighs of relief and murmur things like: "Thanks be to God... ooooh that's lovely... ooooh do it again.... ooooh that's brilliant..."

No matter how closely I listen I cannot hear you breathing as you read these words. I can imagine it though.

Skimming Moos

The whole system is suspect if you ask me. It's perfectly okay to pick up little flat pieces of slate and skim them across the surface of a lake. We did it when we were kids in Malahide. We whizzed them out across the waters of the estuary and counted the skips until the slate finally slowed down and sank. Go out and do it tomorrow. It's great fun.

But doing it with fully-grown trusting cows is a different matter. It has come to my notice that big strong burly farmers are picking cows up by the tail and swinging them around over their heads. That in itself is bad enough. But when the cow is whizzing around so dizzily that it becomes a brown and white blur, the farmer sends the unfortunate bovine skittering away across the surface of inland lakes and waterways.

They say that it is an exhilarating sight and perhaps it is. For my own part I have no desire to watch a noble cow called Ermintrude or Emily skimming and skipping at high speed towards the opposite bank. Sometimes the cows are so disorientated that they do it on one leg while releasing a terror-stricken MOOOO at the same time. Surely to God we can come up with a more humane way of producing skimmed milk than this. Perhaps at some time in your life you have jumped from a moving train while it is slowing down beside a platform. When you land you have to keep running for a while so that you don't fall and break your neck. It is exactly the same for a cow as it hurtles towards the shore. When it touches land it has to keep on running for a while. In order to get the skimmed milk at its very finest it is apparently crucial that the farmer does the fingering and the squeezing into a silver bucket while the cow is still in transit.

Reliable friends of mine who have hidden in bushes are giving me the most amazing reports of livestock hurtling ashore and being hotly pursued across the fields by agricultural men brandishing three-legged stools and buckets.

If those guys in Brussels called Jacques and Butros Ditto hear about this they will take back all the money they gave us to install symphony orchestras in our milking sheds, and quite right too.
As far as I am concerned, cows are for munching grass and swishing their tails at flies and rubbing up against trees whenever they are itchy. Cows are for completing statements like "How now brown ..." and for jumping over the moon whenever they feel so inclined. They haven't got the faintest idea about skimming over lakes. It is not in their nature. I am not for one moment condoning this practice, but if we are going to continue, it might be a compassionate gesture to fit them with skis and nice coloured helmets.
Oh and another thing. I have seen goalposts on television during rugby matches and they are profusely padded in case the players crash into them. My friends who hide in bushes have seen actual instances of skimmed milk cows careering across lakes and whamming into trees on the opposite bank This is not good for tourism. Or Ermintrude. Or Emily. Let us pad the trees. Or the cows. Or both.

Sheep-Chasing Oak Trees

"Dear Lord — I have never asked you for very much, so please send me a man with no bad habits, a flat stomach and a private invome," prayed Regina Carmody. She sat under a shady tree, contemplatively chewed a daisy and waited for a heavenly response.

High above in the leafy branches Nathan Quixby was so finely balanced that the turbulence set up by a passing sparrow knocked him from his perch. As he crashed through the foliage he idly thought, "I wonder who I'll hit this time," because the great man was forever falling out of trees. It was a family failing.

Regina glanced up and gasped, "God — that was quick!" She would have thought a lot of other things as well if Nathan's left boot had not struck her right temple a glancing blow which rendered the poor girl unconscious. She deserved better.

Nathan was aghast. "Not again," he groaned. His life seemed to be an ongoing series of high branches, passing sparrows and unconscious females. Perhaps he was suffering from a chemical imbalance or something. I'm not really sure.

The paramedics who followed Nathan everywhere speedily resuscitated Regina. She raised herself on one elbow, made firm eye contact with Quixby and said between clenched teeth: "On your bike thou varlet with the bulging stomach before I take a knitting needle to you." Who could honestly blame her? Early next morning Nathan wandered into a nearby village ringing his bell and announced loudly: "OYEZ ... OYEZ ... GIVE ME A COW WHICH HAS DIED FROM NATURAL CAUSES AND I WILL GIVE YOU A MIRACLE!" Normally nobody would have taken a blind bit of notice. Good and true people including myself have found themselves on the wrong side of locked doors for less. But Quixby was brandishing a cheque book and offering dizzy sums of money.

More cows died from natural causes during the next week than at any time since records commenced in 1871. Farmers thronged the main street with tractors and trailers. Some of them even trudged into town with inert cows draped across their shoulders. Quixby was jubilant.

For the next couple of days he carefully removed the motor lobes from the cows' brains and lovingly implanted them into young saplings. Then he set the little trees into the ground and murmured softly, "Let nature take her course".

Some years later Bridie O'Hagan and Micilin Og O'Thwisk were searching each other for tattoos in a haystack when Bridie surfaced for air and was profoundly astonished by what she saw. "Micilin," she shrieked *as bearla*. "As I live and breathe I do perceive an oak tree climbing in over my father's gate!"

"Would you have a bit of sense, Bridie?" he snorted. "Are you at the enchanted turnips again or what?"

Seconds later the terrified pair took to their heels and fled across *An Pairc Fada* with a frenzied tree scampering along on its roots behind them

That was only the start of it. All across the county Quixby's trees were chasing sheep, disrupting funerals and in some extreme cases were stopping Inter-City trains at level-crossings and shaking their branches at the ticket checkers.

"For the love and honour of God, Mister Quixby, would you ever keep your trees on a lead or something?" demanded a Brown Owl whose entire troop of girl

guides had been hunted across a mountain range by a couple of sprightly spruces.
"Build furniture from my trees," urged Quixby. "Consider what a boon it will be for arthritic furniture removers. They will merely shout "HUP, HUP" and a heavy snooker table will scamper up the ramp and into the van all by itself."
I don't know why he bothers.

A Bird's Life

I'm really glad that I'm not a baby bird. I'm sure that it's grand while you're comfy in the nest with lumps of fluff and soft stuff to lie on. That bit I could handle ... no trouble at all.
Everytime you get hungry you open your beak and kick up a row and your mother fills you full of delicious juicy worms. It's the life of Reilly.
At no stage do your parents tell you where you actually are. They don't say things like: "Get those worms down you ... oh and by the way we're living on the edge of a cliff with a sheer drop of 3,000 feet into the Irish Sea." ... or "Try not to over-react, but right now you are on top of a tree in the middle of O'Connell St."
So you snuggle up for the night and you hear th0se distant crashing waves or the sound of young guys kicking the hell out of one another and you say: "Pray tell me mater and pater — what is that?" The only response you get is: "Shut up and finish your worms."
It's not really fair.

The very first time that you peer out over the edge of the nest gives you exactly the same feeling as a bunny rabbit watching a gigantic articulated truck bearing down with headlights blazing and your little furry legs don't work anymore. It is blind vaporising panic.
"Ahhhhhhh!! How the hell did I get up here? Holy shit — it's miles down! We're all going to die ... Ahhhhh!!!"
Straight away your mother tries to defuse your fright by stuffing another beakful of worms down your throat.
"Cut that out mother! Keep those worms to yourself! I want a few straight answers. What the fuck am I doing up here in a tree? Are you all mad or what? God, I can't bear to look." At that traumatic moment you would be infinitely happier as a baby pig or a baby goat or a baby anything else at all. Even a baby human isn't that bad. At least you don't peep over the side of your pram and find yourself stuck on a ledge halfway up Howth Head. My god, it must be terrible. And the worst is yet to come.
"Mother and father, I'm sorry for swearing ... honestly I am. I'll try to be calm, truly I will ... so tell me this and tell me no more ... have we got a nice safe rope ladder for getting up and down from here or what?"
"Eh ... how shall we put this ... those .... those little feathery yokes you've got there ... wings .... that's what we call them ... me and your daddy ... they're called wings. You see ... you sort of dive out of the nest and you flap them up and down and you whizz through the air and ah ... you fly."
"Ahhhhh! Help! Somebody help me! I've got mad parents! They want me to jump out of here! We're all going to die! Ahhhh ! ! !"

Release The Grindle!

I propose to use the word 'grindle' instead of 'penis' during this piece, because if you use the word 'penis' more than ten times on one page you will go straight to hell when you die. So grindle it is.

I certainly don't blame Almighty God when I catch my grindle in my zip. It is not my Creator's fault. He didn't invent zips. When He endowed Adam with a grindle it was His intention that we would spend the rest of our days running around quite happily in the Garden Of Eden with our grindles flapping freely in the wind. Then Adam screwed us all by munching a Granny Smith, and he was fired out into exterior darkness where, not content to leave well enough alone, he went and invented the zip fly. Then the trouble started.

When you catch your grindle in a zip it hurts like hell. It is possibly the most excruciating agony known to man apart from getting a belt of a football amidships. When your grindle gets pinched you feel like yelling at the top of your voice: "ARRRRRRGGG!" or words to that effect. But being a man you are not supposed to react or flinch when agony hits you. I saw a man recently on a bus who whacked his head against the bar when he stood up. He didn't shriek "YEOOOOW!" or anything. He smiled. I swear it. The man whammed his head against cold metal and he smiled. That is what you do when you are cool and laidback and male. Pain doesn't cost you a thought.

So you stand there in a public convenience with your unfortunate grindle gripped between the teeth of your

zip and you smile casually at the man who is wee-weeing beside you. Even though your eyes are watering and agony messages are screeching up to your brain, you smile and say, "That's not such a bad day now, sure it's not."
To the best of my knowledge there are no training courses available for men which teach you how to release your grindle without tripling the pain. I believe that FAS should run a special course on 'Painless Grindle Releasing'. I would be the first to join.
Years ago when I was little, I remember the pain involved in pulling a strip of Elastoplast off my arm. I peeled it up slowly inch by inch and little hairs pinged out by the roots and my eyes watered and I smiled because I was male. Then my mother suddenly created a diversion. She pointed in the opposite direction, asked "What's that?", I looked over and she whipped off the plaster so quickly it was all over before I knew it.
Unfortunately you can't ask the man weeweeing beside you to create a diversion like that while he unexpectedly whips your grindle free. Irish Catholics have been sent across the Alps on their bare knees for less.
This is why I propose to become 'Zippie Man'. I shall have a big 'Z' emblazoned secretly on my chest. I shall pose as Cecil O'Hara, mildmannered bank official and I won't even say boo to a goose. But whenever the "Z" sign appears in the sky I shall dive headfirst into the nearest clump of bushes, whip off my suit and fearlessly become "ZIPPIE MAN!!!"
From this moment on, mankind has got nothing to fear. I pledge my life to that most worthy, noblest of causes...

setting grindles free. Wherever a trapped grindle brings tears to the eyes, there shall you find Zippie Man. I shall crash in through the window yelling: "What's that?" and pointing dramatically in the opposite direction. Before you even know it, your grindle shall be released and I will be gone again before you've got the chance to ask an old lady in a flowery bonnet: "Who was that man with the 'Z' on his chest?" She would most probably respond in an emotional whisper: "Tell your grandchildren that was no ordinary mortal... THAT WAS ZIPPIE MAN!!!"

I shall not charge you any money. My reward shall be the knowledge that once again your grindle is free to flip and flop and flap and do all the multifarious things which grindles love to do... YAHOOO!!!

Battle Of The Bulge

I never thought it would happen. I used to have a lovely flat undulating stomach. None of it bulged or stuck out or anything. Women used to say: "My goodness — just look at that definitive man over there. Isn't that the flattest stomach you ever did see?" They used to stand beside me on buses and rub up against it. They used to come up to my flat stomach and paint pictures on it with their fingers using pineapple yoghurt and chocolate sauce. It was brilliant.

I was only saying to my stomach the other day: "I don't know what's wrong with you. My ears and my nose and my toes... they're perfectly happy as they are. You don't see them getting all bulgy and wobbly so what the hell is the matter with you?" My stomach said nothing. It knows bloody well that it has profoundly betrayed me. Sometimes I am standing in a bus queue and a really attractive slender young woman comes towards me. I find myself taking a very deep breath and drawing the whole edifice inwards. I reduce my outward body size by about ten per cent. The tension and the effort and the stress is unbelievable.

Professor Rufus Thwisk has asked a question which has put the fear of God into me. Addressing a recent World Seminar on Wobbles, Bulges and Flops he said: "When a man pulls his stomach inwards, where exactly does it go? It certainly doesn't come out again at the back because we would see it if it did. We would exclaim: 'Good heavens just look at that man over there with a stomach where his back should be!'"

Thwisk believes that a retracted stomach actually forces its way into your legs. It pushes all the stuffing downwards with great pressure towards your feet. He has issued this timely warning: "Should the downward pressure inside your legs become too great there is an ever-present risk that you will blow your feet to bits."

I like to believe that he only said this to get his name in the papers. Nonetheless he is advocating a remarkable new pioneering operation for men with mountain ranges where their stomachs used to be.

"The time has come to check out the feasibility of hollow legs. I'm not saying that we should take out all the stuffing because obviously your legs would cave in and then where would you put your trousers? But it is crucial that we make some space available before we are faced with the phenomenon of exploding feet and bits of shoe leather flying in all directions."

Some married men are now claiming the right to engage in extra-marital frolics with their stomachs. Cillian Mac an Bhosca Mhoir Bhain is spokesperson for the newly formed 'Unmarried Wobble, Bulge And Flop Society'. His assertion is simple. "In many cases a bulging stomach took no part whatsoever in the marriage ceremony because it wasn't there at the time. Therefore our members claim that their subsequent bulges and wobbles are single. However, their partners have got no real need to worry because there isn't a lot you can do with your stomach anyway apart from the creative use of mayonnaise, sardines and rhubarb juice."

I want somebody to do press-ups and sit-ups for me. Whenever I attempt them for myself, my head goes all black and dizzy and I see coloured lights which crackle with static and whizz around behind my eyes. Then I nearly die. Medical science has come a long way. It is now possible to make a cow pregnant ten thousand miles away from a bull. Hip replacements are ten a penny. Surely it is possible to come up with a series of tubes and wires and sensors which I can attach to a really fit person who can lie on the floor beside me and do all the energetic bits on my behalf while the benefits are transferred to me.

Perhaps we can manufacture special bottles of Tippex For Unwanted Tummies. Perhaps we can manufacture special bottles of Tippex For Use on Burnt Toast. Perhaps my granny was secretly a Romanov. Yahooooo!

Caution —Tomcats Spraying

Tomcats love to back up against things and spray them. It's a marvellous system really. They leave powerfully pungent messages on bushes, hedges and garden poles. "Now see here Ginger or whatever your name is... just you set foot on my path again and I'll send you home minus more than your whiskers." The system works just fine as long as Willow and Hoot scent the great outdoors with their messages to the world.

But then Willow figured out that everytime I go away to do a gig I bring my black shoulder bag with me. So he hit it with a supercharged slow-acting spray which only works on Express Buses. The heaters activate it and it gradually permeates the entire bus. Essence of Willow wafts up around people while they wrinkle their nostrils and try to figure out how in hell did a tomcat manage to sneak on board without paying the driver.

Hoot prefers to zap the curtains. Everything about him is concentrated. When he purrs, his whole body vibrates and his whiskers tremble and I swear that he uses Duracell batteries in his purring box. When he sprays indoors all of my potted plants implode and the Superser spontaneously lights itself.

Sometimes I catch him in the nick of time. He is going into reverse with the look of rapt concentration which immediately precedes the spraying mode. It is crucially important to grab him and make it to the front door before he starts his State of the Nation address. It is even more important to keep him pointing away from you. Tomcats operate on the Magnus Magnusson principle

of "I've started so I'll finish." They simply don't have an off-switch.
Cats also suffer from involuntary chattering. If they spot a robin or a sparrow they just can't help themselves. Their teeth chatter wildly and make a demented sort of 'ang ang ang' noise and if you were a little bird it would scare the living shite out of you. I'm not too sure what the 'angs angs' actually mean, but I'm convinced that the words 'Chef's Special' are in there somewhere.
Jasper Thwisk the Elder maintains that cannibals used to chatter 'ang, ang, ang' messages before dining on evangelists. We'll just have to take the man's word for it.
I think that interaction between the sexes would be a lot clearer if we all suffered from involuntary chattering as well. It would eliminate all the cool dude stuff. If a man sees a woman and he feels attracted to her his teeth start to go 'ang ang ang' and straight away she knows. If she fancies him as well she 'angs angs angs' in perfect harmony and they are cleared for immediate take-off. It might be confusing in a crowded pub on a Saturday night if twenty or thirty people are wildly chattering at the same time but as Jasper Thwisk the Younger observes "As long as you don't intend eating anybody there is no real harm done." It's true for him.

Cat Notes

It is entirely up to yourself whether or not you let a cat sleep under the bed covers at night. There is a lot to be said for it during the winter. You don't have to fill them

up with hot water, they don't lose their heat, and there is no danger of the stopper coming out and making your duvet all soggy.
Cats, however, are very adept at farting noiselessly in their sleep. I don't know how they do this. I think it dates back to early Egyptian times, but I'm not really sure. Jasper Thwisk the Twin believes that this is how cats talk and sing in their sleep. After one particularly impassioned aria by Hoot I was obliged to spring out of bed and open every window in the house. All of my blue-tacked posters curled upwards and the fridge defrosted itself in ten seconds. Hoot was still sound asleep, so I covered him with a cardboard box and took a sleeping bag up to the attic.
Sometimes I sing to Willow: "If you're happy and you know it, do a meow." And by God he does. I didn't teach him or anything. He just does it. It's wonderful, it's innocent and it's true. Yahoo!

Buzzing On The Street

I haven't felt so gloriously happy and blissfully free for a very long time. For the last five lazy lingering weeks I've been sitting in North Earl Street on a lovely little red canvas chair, drinking coffee, reading Oscar Wilde, getting a brilliant sun tan and selling oodles of copies of my new poetry book.
I'm not gigging or broadcasting or anything like that. I'm simply sitting there enjoying a complete absence of tension and anxiety and all the other crappy negative feelings which stop you from singing your head off first

thing in the morning. Every so often somebody asks me to mind a bike for a while or keep an eye on a baby in a buggy, but sure you'd do that in your sleep.

It seems to bother some people when they see me grooving in my chair and yawning lazily. "A person of your stature shouldn't be out in the street lessening his reputation like this." That is exactly what one man said to me. I found his words so funny and so sad that I wrote them into my jotter. "Have you sunk this low?" I swear to you. This is what another man said. "Jesus Pat, are things that bad?" A third man asked me that.

"You have it handy sitting there you lucky bastard." I don't think he approved either.

Every single day brings very many good people who stop and talk to me about my work. They encourage me and nourish my spirit. Real people who don't read elitist poetry magazines, who couldn't give a shite about "The Arts", who don't need shiny polished men in suits to tell them what is good poetry and what isn't. They know what they like and they like my work and I feel very proud. One woman telling me that my poems helped her through a very traumatic period in her life means i n f i n i t e l y more to me than the 'J. Arthur Somebody or Other Poetry Prize'.

American tourists like to take my picture and anything else that is free. They like to pick up the book, read it from cover to cover, say how brilliant it is and then put it down again.

One teenage girl stopped and told me, "Our class was talking about you in school. Most of us loved your stuff;

but one girl said 'He's only a reject from the Sixties who got lost.' The teacher was raging." Yippee!

A man who I last met in my poetry group in prison stopped to talk for a while. He is now free, vulnerable and broke. He came back ten minutes later with a little fluffy kitten which he bought for me in a Pound Shop. It means more to me than anything else that has happened on the street this summer.

"Are you Lee Dunne? I love your plays." A grey-haired woman said that to me, so I made her deeply happy by signing a piece of paper: "Lots of love to you Nellie from Lee."

She was thrilled.

Another man paid me what I think is some sort of compliment. "I just want to say I agree with you on the telly and that. People think you're an idiot and that... you know." Five minutes later a woman paused, looked up and down the street to check that none of her friends could see her talking to me. "I just want to tell you," she said, "You are absolutely wrong about everything." I wrote that in my jotter as well.

I find it a wonderfully liberating feeling not to have a job, not to have to be anywhere at a given time, not to have to be nice to people who I can't stand. I thank God for blessing me with a great deal of talent and all the time in the world to waken in the morning with a song on my lips, fill a sack full of books and get the bus downtown to offer my truest thoughts in print to anyone who wishes to stop, have a chat, mind my chair while I nip into Madigans for a quick wee wee, tell me I'm right, tell me I'm wrong, have a free read, seduce me with their eyes, buy me a can of orange or ask me to lend them a pound. God is good, Dublin is great and I feel free... YIPPEEE!

Silly Soccer Season

I believe that it is very unfair to ask any man to stand in a human wall during a soccer match. A high-speed leather ball hitting you squarely in the pleasure centre could raise your voice by a hundred octaves and have you walking like Quasimodo for the rest of your life.

I propose that we provide each team with a good strong polystyrene wall on wheels which can be trundled out whenever it is needed. The lads can crouch down behind it safe and sound and secure in the knowledge that their respective nuts will not be pulverised by a leather projectile. There can be nice little peepholes in the wall so that the lads can peer through and see what is going on.

I only went to a Republic of Ireland international game once in Lansdowne Road. A glossy, sophisticated Brown Thomas lady with sunglasses on the top of her head asked me: "Which one is Tony Cascarino?" So I pointed to Paul McGrath and explained: "There really isn't any Tony Cascarino. He doesn't actually exist. It's just a name which the FAI make up to keep the Irish/Italian community happy. All the lads take turns at pretending to be him, and today it's Paul McGrath's turn." This information added greatly to her enjoyment. I couldn't take Lansdowne Road seriously after that.

I don't think that we need commentators or experts at all. Each player can shout his name out really loud every time he touches the ball. Then we'll all know exactly who he is. He can also shout out interesting little biographical details about himself, and if his mother happens to have a shop he can shout out her 'Mega-Deals' as well. It's only right.

I do not think that spectators should shout deeply upsetting things at referees and linesmen, especially if they happen to be bald. These men have got feelings too. I don't care what anybody says, there is no possible justification for roaring: "Go home you baldy blind bollix" at anyone. Alliteration is no defence.

I have seen perfectly respectable family men transformed into raving frenetic personality disorders who vent their fury on some innocent match official's shiny bald head. They shout and roar and their spit flies in all directions. I would suggest that this is baldism at its very worst. If they have to shout something, how about — "Oh noble referee with the distinguished receding hairline... with respect, I feel that thou art slightly in error."

People who stay at home and only ever watch soccer on television will never fully realise how much they are missing. Commentators are forever saying things like "That Roy Keane does a lot of invaluable work off the ball," but unless you actually attend a match you will never see it because the cameras always follow the action.

When the ball was at the far end of the pitch for example, Packy Bonner liked to sit in the back of his net

and hand-crochet purple woolly hats for old ladies to fling onto the stage during Daniel O'Donnell concerts. Packie also recycled teabags for the foreign missions, and embalmed dead earwigs for generations yet to come.
Denis Irwin, on the other hand, prefers to take out his penknife and carve tasteful scenes from the Kama-Sutra onto the corner flag.
Liam Brady never really fitted into Jack Charlton's plans because when he was off the ball he loved excavating deep holes in the pitch with a shovel and searching for moles. Foreign groundsmen used to give out hell about this, especially when it rained, because Mick McCarthy would then float his decoy ducks in the resulting pond and blow his wooden quacker. So they had to go.
Adidas are now working on a revolutionary new football boot which doesn't need a player inside it at all. These boots are fully capable of playing a match on their own. The obvious advantages are the significant saving in wages and hotel expenses because these boots would be more than happy to spend the night before the game in a comfy shoe box. Hip hip hooray! Up Bohs!

Jigs, Reels And Flasbacks

You get tons of medals for doing it. There is no other dance form known to man or woman for which you get so many ribbons and things. When some Irish dancers venture out of doors wearing all their medals they have to strap on a specially-designed lightning conductor.

Seamus MacMicilin an Bhosca went prancing up the airy mountain with all his jig medals pinned to his chest and was instantly vapourised by an avenging bolt from the heavens. "Take that you vainglorious jigger," said a source close to God.
Siobhan Nic an Iarnrod Fada went gamboling up the rushy glen waving all her medals on a stick and was reduced to a hot hiss of steam by a huge big heavenly finger. "So perish all hornpipey show-offs," said an angel of the Lord. That's what you get.
LSD is a very bizarre sort of a drug because many years after taking it people are still visited by bouncing unicorns and pink-winged horses which prance across the tops of their sugar bowls shouting "Wheee... it's me again."
Irish dancing has the same bewildering effect on little girls who are waiting patiently at bus stops. Hours after the Feis has finished and all the medals have been piled into security vans, the little girls' heads are filled with visions. One minute they are standing at the bus stop saying: "Mammy — why don't we melt down all my medals and build a suspension bridge to the Aran Islands?" Next thing they are doing wild little jigs and reels because phantom ceili bands are invading their heads with red hot diddle-dee-idles.
Sometimes these flashbacks visit old men in their nineties who are crouched in front of turf fires drinking hot cocoa and fondling their next door neighbour's dentures. Next minute they are careering across ploughed fields, leaping nimbly over stone dykes and flinging themselves headfirst into bogholes. We have got to

address this phenomenon immediately because the bogholes are all full.

One thing which the adjudicators insist upon is that you keep both arms locked rigidly against your sides while your jig is in progress. They are not interested in excuses like: "But they were throwing bags of chips at me your honour." Unless you immobilise your top half completely they will unhesitatingly confiscate all your medals and ban your mother from the Mansion House. This voluntary paralysis is causing grave concern to parents because their children frequently arrive home from a Feis in a security van and attempt to open the doorhandles with their teeth.

In its earliest form Irish dancing called for acute muscle control because you were also obliged to keep both legs wedged tightly together and the only part of your body which you were allowed to move was your ears. You weren't even permitted to blink. You stood there utterly immobile and waggled your ears in time to the accordion.

The Annals of Na Fianna are filled with glorious descriptions of highly-charged ear jigs and ear reels. Oisin of the Ambidextrous Ears was so named because on a particularly good day he could perform a rousing reel with his right ear while simultaneously wiggling a wild abandoned hornpipe with his left. "'Tis nothing," he would exclaim modestly. "I inherited it from my mother."

Historians are now inclined towards the belief that the early ear-dancing of Na Fianna flourished mainly because of deep-rooted fear. The punishments for breaches of etiquette were so severe that Oisin fled to Tir na nOg when nobody was looking and took both of his ambidextrous ears with him. If you as much as rippled an arm or a leg during a Fenian Feis they were chopped off instantly with an adjudicator's broadsword. "Take that you dissident leg twitcher," Fionn MacCumhaill would exclaim *as gaéilge* with a graceful swipe of his Sword of Light and limbs would fly in all directions. Many Fenians gave up dancing altogether and started burying chalices instead. I don't need to do Irish Dancing. My left arm is paralysed anyway.

Has Your Husband Started This Carry-On Yet?

He read about alternative medicine. One book described how a surgeon went through the motions of performing an operation. He simply did all the actions over the patient's stomach with his hands as if he was miming it. No incision of any kind was made yet the desired effect took place inside the patient. Kevin Hahesy was profoundly impressed.

"Hmmmmm," he said.

Next morning his wife asked him what he'd like for breakfast.

"Alternative eggs and bacon will be grand, thanks, Brigid," he said. "Oh, and I won't need a knife and fork."

Kevin's wife watched in wide-eyed silence as he sat down at an empty table and licked his lips.

"By God, Brigid," he said. "That bacon smells lovely."

The frying pan was still hanging up on the back of the kitchen door. Kevin sprinkled invisible salt and pepper over a breakfast which hadn't been prepared yet.
"You can't beat a good feed first thing in the morning," he said and lashed into his alternative bacon and eggs. "Eh, I'm not sure how this will sound to you," he continued. "But the breakfast would taste even better if you went through the motions of actually preparing it first ... you know ... sort of wave your hands around a bit over the frying pan and make lots of sizzily sounds with your mouth."
Brigid nodded weakly and sat down. Her life assumed a strange dream-like quality as she watched her spouse holding the kettle underneath the tap and making a noise like splashing water. Then he stood beside it for a while and made very busy boiling sounds. Almost in spite of herself, Brigid sprinkled alternative coffee into an invisible mug with a non-existent spoon. Kevin filled it up from the empty kettle and wrinkled his nostrils.
"Hmmmm," he said. "There's an aroma for you — will you have a mug yourself while I'm at it?" Brigid spoke with a voice which she didn't recognise as her own and said: "I think I'd better let you make your own lunch."
A close friend called around to Brigid for a chat at mid-morning. "Is ... is there something the matter?" she asked.
Brigid was moving slowly around the kitchen sweeping the floor with an imaginary brush. "Wrong? wrong?" she replied with the sort of voice you use when you're under deep hypnosis. "Yes ... will you have a look at that vacuum cleaner of mine and see if you can get it started?"

Her friend was just about to say "I'd feel an awful lot better if I could even see the sweeping brush."
But Brigid was now putting an even more severe strain on their friendship by making splashing noises into the kettle. Kevin was simultaneously freaking out the office by lashing into his alternative sandwiches.
On reflection I think we've still got a very long way to go.

Are You Happy?

People tell you the last thing you need to hear. I said to the man on the bus that I was going to the dentist. "It's not so bad though. I'm only getting a small filling."
"That's what the cousin said. Only a small filling. You never saw so much blood. A main artery."
"But there's no arteries in your teeth."
"No but the dentist hit a nerve and the cousin's leg shot up in the air. He's double-jointed so his foot flew back at an angle and booted the dentist's drilling hand. Before you could say 'Pelican House', the drill rebounded off the ceiling like a heat-seeking missile and harpooned the jugular. A small filling is right."
I told a man on another bus that I was going out to Beaumont Hospital for a little bit of physiotherapy. "They're going to put a very mild current of electricity through my arm to try and get it moving again."
"Is any of your underclothing damp?"
"Not as far as I know".
"They don't mix: water and electricity. The woman down the road was having the same thing done for a stiff

finger. A rigid digit, the doctor called it. Her vest was damp and when the current went through her finger, all her underclothing started to smoulder. The physiotherapist didn't smell the thermals scorching because she had a head-cold. Only for a porter who was passing and said: "I think that woman is starting to go up in smoke.," — she'd have gone home in an urn. Take my advice and make sure your vest is dry."

I told a man how happy I was feeling.

"Things are going great right now. I feel in top form."

"That's how it starts. Mind you, they can control it with medication if they catch it in time."

"But I feel fabulous".

"So did the brother-in-law. Not a bother on him. He never spotted the elation either. Before you know where you are you'll be selling your house to the milkman for 75p, swopping your car for a copy of 'The Beano' and sitting up a tree in Fairview Park at 3.30 in the morning singing 'Oh Happy Day'. If I was you I'd start thinking good healthy depressing thoughts right now before you O.D. on happiness. Top form is right."

I'm not telling a soul about my corn. I don't want to hear about chainsaws, nitro-glycerine, lethal lasers, chiropodists with dyslexic scalpels or damp vests. There's great comfort in silence.

Our Gardai Deserve Better Than This!

It's certainly nothing new. Pliny the Elder wrote about Greek scholars whose legs crackled and sparked in company. Plutarch chronicles the case of Roman senators who "didst most mysteriously scorch their togas from within." And still it happens.

Three weeks ago Garda Risteard Heffernan was on routine foot patrol in Mount Street. It was a clear misty night. In his 9.30 call to HQ he reported a faint smell of burning. "Am going to investigate," he said. His 9.33 call added that it was a curious case of scorching — "because no matter where I go it is still in the vicinity". His 9.35 call was succinct and to the point. "Me trousers are ablaze — am about to leap into the canal near Baggot Street." The splash and the hiss of steam were timed at 9.355 precisely.

The Institute for Research and Standards dried out the trousers and subjected them to rigorous tests. They discovered a very high presence of Dacrylon in the fabric. Garda Heffernan then signed a consent form. Highly confidential tests on his legs followed. These proved conclusively that inter-action between hairs on men's legs and the suspect fibre can lead to overheating — and, in the case of Garda Heffernan, to leaping into canals. Whether or not this happens is entirely dependent on the tensile strength of each hair. A hair with a breaking point of .0654 grammes or over is seriously at risk.

The institute issued a list of persons who are wearing what they termed "High Risk Trousers". It included gardai, customs officials, busmen and the lads who tear cinema tickets in half.

It was then recommended that until the trousers could be de-sparked, all those in the "high risk" category should shave their legs and submit to weekly tensile strength tests.

The outcry was fierce. "Surely an Irishman's legs are a matter between himself, his wife and his conscience," said a source close to indignation.

CIE made matters worse by recommending that their bus inspectors should in future either wear a fire-extinguisher strapped to the waist or keep strictly to bus routes which run parallel to inland waterways and rivers. "There is no call for unreasoning panic," said Doctuir Breffni O Aonghusa at the Institute. "We have just perfected a modified tyre-pressure gauge. On-the-spot tensile checks are now a reality."

"He's not coming near me with one of them yokes," said a Customs official. "That sort of behaviour wrecked Sodom and Gomorrah." Six people have applied independently to the IDA for small industry grants. They plan to establish asbestos tights factories. This the sort of forward thinking that can still make Ireland great.

How The Pint Drinkers Were Saved

You won't find many publicans like him. He realised that some men's stomachs were coming between them and their pints. The sort of men who had extended their natural boundaries outwards and frontwards and now they couldn't stand up at the counter. There was a gap between them and their pints.

Montiverdi Hegarty saw the pain in their eyes. He was a caring publican.

"Hail to thee, oh men, with the wobbling edifices," he said. "I realise full well what ails thee. Why dost thou not stand sideways on to the bar?"
And they tried it. But this formed a solid wall of stomachs and nobody else could get anywhere near the counter.
"Aw now lads," one regular complained. "Yis'll have to put them stomachs somewhere else — yiz have built up an impenetrable barrier of wobble."
Some of the more extreme cases were able to balance their pints on top of their fronts so that their stomachs formed a natural kind of a counter. But the others were desolate. "Are we condemned to spend the rest of our lives distanced from our pints?" they wailed. "Supposing," said Montiverdi, "supposing the counter was on a level with your necks and the top of it extended outwards like a shelf. I'll get it hinged and I'll set your pint glasses securely into it. Once every minute it will tilt automatically towards you and you can sup your pints."
The stomach men were jubilant. Montiverdi was a man of his word. One half of the counter was raised to neck level as promised. It jutted out just like he'd said. And once every minute it tilted. But the lads had second thoughts.
"This is all very well," they said. "But every time ye go to the Gents ye miss a couple of tilts And anyway it now means that we're all drinking at the same speed." And no matter how much the glass tilts there's always a bit at the bottom we can't get at ... the whole arrangement is cat."

The solution was as simple as it was obvious. Firstly the counter was restored to its normal height. Then Montiverdi had stomach alcoves cut into it. But the sections were not removed. They remained as part of the counter. Gently spring-loaded like the leaves that slide in and out of a dining room table. Concave. You simply leaned your stomach against them and they moved inwards forming a personalised alcove.
Some of the men wanted the alcoves numbered and season tickets issued. That's the sort of thinking that gave them the stomachs in the first place.

Making Money From Your Asthma!

We were bored stiff. Eight men in a public ward in hospital last week.
Then the doctor scratched each of my arms six times and introduced twelve different substances into the scratches. House dust mite into one. Cow's milk into another. Straw dust and so on. " If you are allergic to any of these substances," he said, "your arm will react at the appropriate scratch." Then he was gone.
The men surrounded my bed and looked at my arms. "There's money to be made out of them scratches," one of them said. And he took out a pound. "I'll have a quid on that scratch there — a pound says that'll be the first one to react." Another man made a close examination of my left arm. "That's a fierce class of a scratch altogether," he said. "A fiver on that one." Money began

to pile up on my locker and the whole thing was getting out of control.
Then the man with the appendix took over. He used to work on the tote so he had an instinct for this sort of thing. "All right lads — form a line and have your money ready. Pound bets on the right arm — the left one is reserved for five pound bets only." He numbered each of my scratches with a biro and gave out official receipts on a prescription pad.
Word spread to the other wards. Men clutching pound notes hobbled in on crutches. A woman in a wheelchair whizzed to the top of the queue with the excuse that her brakes weren't working. A man who hadn't spoken in two weeks because he was suffering from severe shock said in a clear voice: "A tenner covers all the scratches on his right arm with the winnings credited to his left."
A nurse pronounced him cured and he was given back his clothes. The man with both legs on traction was unanimously chosen to hold the money on the grounds that he wasn't going anywhere or likely to be for weeks.
It was at this stage that I wanted to go asleep. The asthma had me worn out.
'Sorry Pat," said the clerk of the course, "there's a lot of money riding on them arms of yours. Nobody sleeps till we get a result." Then someone said: "Supposing he gets a sudden relapse. He'd be whisked off to intensive care — scratches and all. Then where'd we be?"
So it was decided to let me sleep on one condition. That I left my arms out over the covers where the stewards could watch them.

The cheers woke me at twenty past eleven. The arm suddenly flared up. House dust mite was the winner at 4/1. Three people divided the prize money.
The clerk of the course opened up his pyjamas jacket and contemplated his appendix scar. "We'll get some kind of a forecast going on that in the morning," he said. And everybody went to bed happy.

Will I Ever Forget?

A woman on the bus got the ball rolling. She said she was going downtown to buy a pair of boots with her bingo winnings.
"Both of my feet is different," said the man beside her. "All me other parts match perfectly but not the feet ... they're different." He said that he can't get a pair of shoes to fit both feet any more. "Not since they took the X-ray machines out of the shoeshops." I had completely forgotten them. My mother used to bring me into a shoeshop in Talbot Street. You tried on the new shoes and stood up on it. Then you inserted both feet into the base and the shop assistant, your mother and yourself took turns at peering down through the periscope at a fluorescent green X-ray picture of your feet. You could see all your bones clearly.
"It was just like buying your shoes in a hospital outpatients," said the bingo woman. "But they had to get rid of it because half of Dublin was walking around with radioactive feet."

"Luminous socks," said the man beside her. "The Teddy-boys used to wear them. They had radioactive feet as well. It's not generally known — but Dublin predated Chernobyl by about thirty years."

"Girls walking backwards in the pictures," said another man. "They're gone, too." He said that he hasn't had a decent ice-cream in a cinema since the girls stopped walking backwards down the aisles at the interval. "They'd be shining a torch onto their tray and illuminating the ice-cream so you knew what you were getting."

The bingo woman said it was no bad thing that the ice-cream girls were gone. "One of my nieces used to do it," she said. "But she got into such a habit that when she was going up for Holy Communion on Sunday morning she'd be walking backwards towards the altar and her mammy would be hissing at her from the back row: 'Turn around Margaret-Rose ... turn around ... you're making a holy show of us.'"

The man beside her said it's all the one which way you approach Almighty God. "You can be standing on your head for all He cares. Funny all the same ... the way He made your feet different."

"Machines on railway stations ... you could print your name on a strip of metal ... all gone ... ink wells in your desk at school with sludgey stuff on the bottom ... splitting the nib of your pen and writing double ... indicators that flipped up out of the side of your car ... the milkman's horse splashing wee wee onto the roadway ... where is it now ... all gone ..."

"Still and all," said the man with the odd feet. "The radiation in Talbot Street is gone too ..." We all felt better then. So did our feet.

What Can You Do With Your Body?

I never went public on it before. It seemed to be such an insignificant trifle. I assumed that everybody could do it. Push your ear lobe in and out to produce a click which sounds like a bus inspector clipping the tickets. Then I was in my sister's house one night last week. One of my nieces was moving her nose from side to side so that she made a noise which I'd long since forgotten. When we were kids we used to wedge a piece of cardboard against the spokes of our bike. My niece's nose made a noise like the bike in motion when she moved it very quickly from side to side. Then we did a duet. Me ramming my ear lobe in and out and her moving her nose from side to side. It was immensely satisfying.

Suddenly I was looking at people in a completely different light. Looking at them and thinking "I wonder what you can do." I did my ear for a man in the GPO. We were stuck in a stamp queue and he looked very bored. "By God, Pat," he said. "That's amazing. Now you have a listen to this." He moved his stomach in and out with sudden abrupt jerks and then just as suddenly he stopped. A series of rumbles and growls and turbulence followed. Now he swayed his stomach rhythmically from side to side. The sound that he produced reminded me of holding one of those rubber hot-water bottles and sloshing it up and down. He gave me three

marks out of ten and I gave him eight. It seemed only fair.
A woman on the bus did a great one for me. She twisted her mouth to one side so that her right cheek was as taut as a bodhran. Then she played 'The Bells of the Angelus' for me by whacking her hand against the side of her face. The man who was sitting in front of us turned around with a biro in his hand. He played most of 'The Harp That Once Thro Tara's Halls' by banging it against his teeth. "I can't get all the notes anymore because I had two extractions last month," he said.
You would be amazed if you only knew what the man in the street is capable of. A great way to start the ball rolling is for you to do something first. I did my ear lobe for a man in a restaurant yesterday. His response was immediate. "I can only do this once," he said. "Because after that it hurts." There and then he twisted his right leg up behind his head. It seemed to be made of India-rubber. His wife was astonished. "I never knew you could do that," she said. I thought that his reply was just a little bit sad. "You never asked me," he replied.
Ask your marital partner today. "What can you do in the line of ear lobe and nose clicks?" You may well add a whole new dimension to your relationship.

Please Be Gentle With Your Bald Spot

The front bit is fine. I still don't have to comb my hair in about six different directions at once. The front is fine. But the bit at the back is starting to let the sun get in. I noticed it first during the heatwave this summer.

God, I thought the back of my head is roasting ... perhaps it's running a localised temperature or something. I inspected the area very tentatively with my fingers. Hey, I thought, my fingertips are sending back false information to my brain. I couldn't possibly be feeling sunburn back there ... that's where my hair is. A little boy behind me on the bus clinched it. " Mammy — why is the back of that man's head all red?" His mother told him to shut up and read his comic. "Mammy," he insisted. "Look ... now it's getting redder." Suddenly I didn't feel like the only guy from my class in school who'd kept his looks any more. A bald spot ... oh my God ... they'll surely whip me out of the Wax Museum now.

Why did nobody tell me? At least when your fly is open, people talk to you about it in code. They mutter things to you about cheese being on your chin. But bald spots are different. Nobody tells you anything. Why can't they have a coded message about that too. Why can't they mutter: "there's an entire ham omelette on the back of your head?"

Then I remembered the gig in the National Concert Hall a couple of weeks ago. There I was strutting around the stage feeling world famous. And all the time. the audience up at the back ... the high seats directly behind the stage ... they had grandstand view of it. They saw a freshly uncovered bit of me that I had never set eyes on. I didn't even know it was there. The moment of truth with two mirrors was devastating. Would you look at that? The hidden me. I've had that bit for forty-seven years and all the time it's been under wraps. Secret skin.

I wonder how it's feeling now. Flushed out into the open. It's probably terrified. Like one of those nightmares you have about being stranded in the middle of O'Connell Street without even a figleaf for cover.
My bald spot probably needs intensive post trauma counselling. But if I tell my psychiatrist that, he'll surely start lowering his voice and showing me lots of coloured ink-blots. I don't want to go down that road again thank you very much. I'm going to counsel it myself. It's not every day that your body reveals a brand new bit to you. The very least you can do is make it feel like one of the gang. So bald spot ... if you're listening ... welcome to my body ...

Would You Wear A Nightie Like This?

Up to now, we've had nothing to hide. No secrets worth stealing. Up to recently we haven't been subjected to mysterious submarines sniffing around our coasts. Men called Boris, Istvan and Vladimir haven't been lurking behind potted palms in hotel foyers whispering messages to one another.
Somehow the word has leaked out. The Irish are up to something using magnets. For years in our hospitals the nurses have faced huge problems trying to make the bed when the patient can't be moved. Two or three of them have to pitch in and help when the patient is immobile, heaving and straining and counting: "One, two, three, Hup!"
Now for the first time in any country we are experimenting with the Magnetic Nightie ... a revolutionary new

garment which looks and feels like an ordinary night-dress but is impregnated with metallic fibres. When the nurses want to lift a heavy patient they simply wheel in the magnetic canopy which fits easily over the bed like an awning on a four-poster. Then they switch it on and up goes the patient.

Dublin Bus have gone one further. They have discovered how to control magnetism at the precise point where the object leaps forward and attaches itself to the magnet. In other words, the object will follow the magnet while maintaining a constant distance from it. "We hope to use this principle for towing broken-down buses," explained a spokesperson. "No more messing about with tow bars. You simply send out the magnetic tow car and the job is right."

The Department for the Environment still has its doubts. During early Dublin Bus experiments with the tow bus, Pioneer pins and Fáinnes flew out of peoples' jackets, bus stops uprooted themselves while old ladies' shopping trolleys and baby buggies hurtled towards the magnetic field. This was described as a minor teething problem by a spokesperson who wore neither a magnetic nightie, a Pioneer pin or a Fáinne.

The Irish Navy is looking at the notion of building gigantic decoy Blue Whales with a powerful magnetic base. "These can float around the Irish Sea doing no harm to anyone. But if a submarine passes anywhere near one, up she comes. No submarine captain worth his salt wishes to go through his mission stuck to the bottom of a huge Blue Whale."

Boris, Istvan and Vladimir are not their real names.

Where Did You Get My Address?

How do they know where I live? I have never written to them. Yet somehow or other they have got my exact address. American Express, with whom I've never had any contact, have just written to me at my home. I don't like it.

The Reader's Digest have done the same. I've had no contact with them either. Somebody somewhere has furnished them with information which is none of their business. If I wish any company to know where I live I will write and tell them. Otherwise I don't want to hear from them.

The Readers' Digest tried the flattering approach. They wrote and told me that I have been specially selected by them for their offer. Out of all the people who live in my area, they have very carefully chosen me. The whole psychology behind the message is patently transparent. Not everybody measures up to this once-in-a-lifetime offer. But I do. And because I'm so special I'm also in with a chance of a large cash prize if I write back. I didn't feel the least bit flattered or important. I simply felt freaked and thought: "How the hell did you get my address? I never gave it to you."

American Express are willing to help me if I buy a video or new suit and then accidentally damage or lose it. They're offering to leap into the breach if I suddenly need an English-speaking doctor or lawyer in a foreign country. But first they need to know some more things about me besides my address.

How many dependent children have I got? Mind your own business. Am I married or single or other? Mind your own business. Do I own my home or am I renting it? Go and ask somebody else because I'm not telling you. If companies are spreading my home address around, I certainly don't wish to add to their Pat Ingoldsby file.
Too many of you are writing to me and asking me to tell you how long I've been with my present employer? Have I got independent means? Can I supply you with the name of my accountant? Many of you are rounding off your letters to me with facsimile signatures.
If any more of you intend writing to me in the future I want a bit of information as well. To which golf club do you belong? What sort of car do you drive? Is your present marriage a happy one? Have you ever been fired? How much do you earn each year? If you are self-employed I want a statement from your accountant covering your last three years. Are you a real person or is your name the figment of some advertising manager's imagination. Send me these details and maybe we can do business. Oh... send me on your home address while you're at it.

My Left Arm Will Get Me Hanged

My twitch was at me.
I can only take so much tension. Then my left arm starts performing little jerks and dances and leading a strange secret life of its own. That's how I know it's time for a break.

I was queuing in the bank to get some English money. The arm gave a preliminary shudder. It's like a ten-second warning. Then it rose up slowly in front of me and pointed at the ceiling. The teller stopped counting her money to watch. I moved a safe distance away from the queue because sometimes it whacks people on the way down.

"Are you doing yoga or what?" a woman asked me. The arm described a near-perfect arc and returned to base. I rejoined the queue. "It's alright now," I said. "It's gone quiet again."

A man who was getting travellers' cheques stared at it. "What time is it due to go up again?" he asked. I said it was usually about once on the hour, but you can't really depend on it.

He told me the cousin in Kimmage had an arm like that. He had to keep it in his pocket because sometimes it threw things at people. He tried giving it short sharp commands like "Stay!" and "Down!" but found that he only drew attention to himself. So he kept it in the pocket and ate with his fork in his right hand. I told him I was taking my arm for a holiday and he said sometimes you have to do these things. You feel sort of responsible.

I was snoozing in a Pullman seat on the B&I boat. This time there was no early warning. An explosive twitch and the arm was gone before I could grab it. This time it veered sharp left and my hand came to rest in a woman's lap. She looked at it. Then she looked at me. "Take that away this instant or I shall be forced to bite it." I think she meant it.

"It'll move away of its own accord if you leave it for a minute," I told her. She said if she woke Kevin and told him what was after happening, he'd bite more than my hand.
Just then it jerked upwards and hovered uncertainly. I don't think she'd ever seen an arm quite like it before. I explained about the twitch and she promised not to tell Kevin. She said you couldn't read the news on television with that class of a thing. And she slept with one eye open. I think she enjoyed the glorious uncertainty of it all. A detective questioned each passenger as we disembarked at Liverpool. "What is the purpose of your journey sir?"
"I'm taking my left arm up to Scotland for a bit of a rest." He said some women put tartan jackets on their poodles and take them to Milan for the opera. That was far worse.
Sometimes I think that detectives are the only people who understand me.

Pssst...Do You Want A Leaflet?

I WAS determined to get them into the right hands. One thousand leaflets announcing my next poetry reading. None of this standing in the street and dishing them out to the first people who walked past. No way. This batch of leaflets cost me over £80. Each one must go to a trembling poetry fanatic who lies down in front of JCBs to protect an artisan dwelling where James Joyce once crashed out for the night on the sofa.

Standing in Grafton Street monitoring the passers-by, looking out for guys with pony-tails and National Health glasses, dressed in dungarees, with a baby in a canvas sling partially obscuring the 'I Saved A Natterjack Toad' on their tee-shirts. A passing American tourist grabbed a leaflet from my hand and walked on down the street. He was folding it and putting it into his pocket. I raced after him. "Excuse me sir. No offence but would you ever read the bloody thing."

He glanced at it and said he'd be in Paris on that date. "Well then, I want my leaflet back — those yokes cost me eighty pounds." He said I could have it back if I directed him towards some historic sites worth photographing in Dublin. I told him that the perfume counter in Brown Thomas stands on the actual location where Brian Boru was whammed by a Danish axe after the Battle of Grafton Street. I got my leaflet back and Brown Thomas gained a place in Irish history.

"Psssst" I whispered to the three guys who looked like they snorted curry powder in warehouses after dark. "Acid poetry at midnight ... you'll find the address on this. Read it, commit it to memory and eat the leaflet." They walked on very furtively, shielding the leaflet with their bodies and whispering to one another from the sides of their mouths.

The guy who looked like he drove stolen cars three at a time and made withdrawals from other people's current accounts with a pickaxe handle, asked me what the story was, and I told him I was selling four leaflets for a pound. He said rock on brother, keep the head together, watch

out for the law, nice one Pat and if that doesn't work you can always try selling the lighters.
I think there's more money in strawberries but I haven't got a pram.

High As The Night

I'm back in my hotel room now. It's just gone midnight. An exhilarating adrenaline high is surging around inside me. The poetry gig tonight was the best I've done for ages. My whole system is rocking with manic energy. What in the name of God am I going to do until it's time for breakfast? The audience has gone home ages ago. The hotel is quiet. I'm still raring to go.
Wrapping yourself in the white bedsheets and pretending to be the ghost of Christmas past is useless. That only sends you higher because you're still performing. Knocking on the other doors in the corridor and trying to find someone to play 'I Spy With My Little Eye' is no good either. Female guests suspect your motives and the men have usually got important business meetings early next morning. Ringing the night porter and asking him to guess passages out of the bible doesn't work either. They're much too busy.
You prowl around your room and experiment with the light switches. You sit on the floor at 4.30 in the morning and flick the buttons on the television. Most of the stations have gone off the air hours ago. It's now a choice between a basketball match with an Italian commentary or a heavy metal band explaining to a wide-eyed, red-lipped interviewer why the devil isn't

really as bad as some people make him out to be. They maintain that the churches have manipulated the media. It's now 5 a.m. I'm running the bath and pretending to be Ella Fitzgerald by quietly singing 'Manhattan' into the shower fixture.

I haven't got a clue how rock bands handle barnstorming tours of Europe. Twenty or thirty consecutive nights whipping up a frenzy on stage which culminates in a crazy high that as good as leaves you out of your head. I've just done two nights in Irish Art Centres and I'm sitting in a hotel bath at 5.30 a.m. pretending that my big toe is the periscope of a Soviet nuclear-powered submarine and unless I score a direct hit with the soap we're all doomed.

When sleep does come it leaves you in the most unexpected positions. I have wakened up on the floor, in the bath, underneath the bed and half-way down the corridor dressed as the ghost of Christmas Present. On one bewildering occasion I woke up on a sofa in a house in Fermoy. My gig the night before had been in Dingle. If anybody remembers the precise details please write to me. I know nothing.

It's Time To Shake Your Fists In The Air

Some people give out about them. They say that soccer players shouldn't go wild when they score a goal. Pounding the air with their fists. Falling to their knees and disappearing under a flailing avalanche of team mates. Some people think that it's fierce and they're not going to like the subtle spill-over one bit. Already the danger signs are beginning to show.

Last week in a Galway bank one of the tellers was making up his cash at the end of the day. Suddenly he released a passionate whoop and sprang up onto the counter. He waved his hands wildly over his head and yelled:"I've done it... I've done it... I've got a perfect balance!" Then he careered around the building with his jubilant colleagues racing after him. The moment he hit the floor he was buried under an ecstasy of consenting bank officials. The porter was obliged to restore order by whamming them with the contents of a fire extinguisher and shouting: "Easy there lads — the security cameras are still on."

A bus inspector was checking a conductor's waybill on the number 10 bus to the Phoenix Park. You could feel the tension. Little muscles twitched in the conductor's face. Then the inspector initialled the sums and handed the waybill back. All was well. They grabbed each other and the inspector's cap went flying and then the driver hugged the pair of them and for a couple of seconds there were legs and arms everywhere. Passengers stood and cheered and waved scarves over their heads and sang "You'll Never Walk Alone". When the bus reached the Phoenix Park the conductor took off across the grass brandishing his waybill and ran twice around the Zoological Gardens before the passengers got a chance to bundle up on top of him.

Psychologists approve. They talk about sharing one's sense of achievement. Too many people are hiding behind false modesty. They successfully meet a chal-

lenge and then say: "It went well". Yet if they screw something up and make an effortless donkey's hernia out of it they shake their heads and say "I made a haymes of it".
It's time to wave your fists in the air and proclaim: "Yahoo.. I... me... myself... I worked well". Forget all about 'It'. Be like the DART driver who sprang from his cab in Bray last week and fell to his knees on the platform yelling " A great run... on time at every single station!" So many passengers wanted to hop on top of him that he was forced to race up the down line to Wicklow on foot and get the bus home.
The only snag about writing is that it's such a solitary occupation. There's nobody to jump on top of you when you write a good story.

Lament for the Vertical Hold

I used to think that everything in America was either black or white. The sky, the sea, daffodils, grass, fire-engines ... black or white, because that's how we saw them on our first television set. No other colours at all except perhaps a bit of grey. A couple of American tourists came to stay in Malahide around that time, the late fifties, and I couldn't keep my eyes off them. "My goodness," I thought. "They must be really conspicuous at home, with red and green shirts like that they must really stand out."
My father was the one who turned our television set on or off. As head of the household he was the one with the power of "On", "Off", "Change The Stations" or

suddenly terminate a programme in mid-scene with the words: "That is not suitable." So my perception of the world as viewed on a 14" screen was one where colour did not exist and where inhabitants only ever exchanged the briefest of kisses while keeping both feet firmly fixed to the floor.

When the television set was switched on you never knew whether or not you were going to see a clear picture. We'd all be sitting there expecting to witness the Lone Ranger keeping The West safe for old ladies in flowery bonnets and be greeted instead by an awe-inspiring blizzard from which you could hear the occasional gunshot and Tonto muttering: "That is plenty bad Kemo Sabay."

And plenty bad it was too until my father went to work twiddling the rabbit's ears aerial which sat on top of the set. "I can see something! I can see something Dad! I think it's a horse! Left a bit ... left a bit more!"

When the blizzard eventually cleared, my father would still grip the aerial for a while until he felt reasonably sure that The Lone Ranger had come to stay in our sitting room. Then he would walk back away from the set very slowly for fear that any sudden move would plunge the Wild West back into a blizzard from which it might never recover. We all held our breath because we believed that this helped as well.

The tension was still far from finished. If a plane passed overhead or a car stopped outside our house or anyone within a radius of about twenty homes began to dry their hair with an electric dryer, we were right back where we started. We never ever saw any Saturday evening programme which coincided with confessions in the parish church because as soon as the priest pulled his front door behind him and headed down the road with his stole, his housekeeper whammed on the vacuum cleaner. Saturday night confessions always meant a 14 inch blizzard.

Pictures sometimes moved up or down. One minute the action would be centred on our screen and suddenly an entire cattle drive or Bill & Ben, The Flowerpot Men would start heading towards the ceiling or sliding down towards the floor. This was my father's cue to spring from his seat and man the little button known as 'The Vertical Hold'. It was located behind the television so his arm would be stretched around towards the back while he curved the rest of his body forwards so that he could see what was happening on the screen. He twiddled his finger and thumb while the picture spun and whizzed like a manic merry-go-round. "It's slowing down Dad! It's slowing down! You've got it Dad! Hold it … hold it right … there!"

Sometimes people changed shape completely as if we were watching the world inside a fairground distorting mirror.

People's tummies were stretched sideways, their height began to mysteriously double, or the picture began to close in on itself from both sides as if an invisible pair of book-ends was squishing it all up into the middle.

At times like this my father was forced to use both hands at once … he became involved in a very delicate balance between the Vertical *and* the Horizontal hold with both arms wrapped around the set and his head wedged up against the screen. The rest of us sat there and didn't say a word. At times like that there was a profound wisdom in silence.

The Vertical Hold is gone now. So is my father. I miss them both.

Outwitting tbe Bogey-man

Nobody ever told me about the Bogey-man. They didn't have to. There was no official warning or anything like that. We were taught how to use a knife and fork and how to cross the road, but I can't ever remember one significant moment in my early childhood when a parent or a teacher or a garda superintendent took me gently to one side and said quietly, 'What I am about to tell you is for your own good. I have here an identikit picture — millions of children all over the world have helped us to compile it. Look at it very quickly and then look away — don't look for too long or something awful will happen — your nose will start to grow or your ears will drop off. This, my dear child, THIS IS THE BOGEY-MAN!' We just knew. There are certain things that you know as a child without anybody ever telling you. Certain things and places. Places like 'Up in Nelly's Room behind the Wallpaper'. You knew exactly where that was. You could even draw a map. It was a safe place. And Nelly. Nelly would never harm you. Not at all. She was more than happy to live behind the wallpaper and mind things. Things that got lost. Your mother's purse. The front door key. The tin-opener. If they went missing, everybody knew where they were. Behind the wallpaper. Up in Nelly's room. But the Bogey-man. He was different. You knew intuitively that he was only interested in the one thing. He didn't give a hoot about lost objects. He had a sack-a personalised sack with your name on it and he couldn't rest easy until you were in it. He didn't have a wife or a mother or go to the pictures or things like that-he was much too busy monitoringyour movements.

Me and my brother would go upstairs at night and we'd get undressed and we knew exactly how far 'grabbing distance' was from the bed-we got undressed over near the window. That was Stage One. Stage Two involved getting into bed without having your ankles grabbed. One by one, we hurtled across the cold linoleum in our bare feet and took off like Olympic athletes bouncing up off a powerful springboard. We described a perfect arc and crash-landed onto the middle of the mattress—'Phew! That was close!'

My brother always made me sleep on the outside of the bed. He made me lie in the high-risk area while he claimed the safe bit in against the wall.

I'm older than you,' he said. 'When you're older, you sleep on the inside. That's . . . that's how it is.'

There was only one possible avenue of approach and that was up the outside, although as long as you kept your legs in under the covers, you were safe. The Bogey-man had this unwritten code of rules. He never grabbed your ankles when they were in under the covers. He had his own curious sense of ethics. On the one hand, it wouldn't cost him a thought to plunge you head-first into his sack, even on your birthday-it was all the one to him. Yet, at the same time, as long as you kept your legs in under the covers, you were safe. You knew the rules and so did he.

Beds in furniture shops or showrooms didn't interest him. He didn't waste his time lurking under them. Bunk beds-the top half of bunk beds-they were no use to him either. No. He much preferred to lie under mine, directly under my half, waiting patiently for me to fall asleep . . . waiting patiently for an unguarded leg.

Sometimes I would awaken in the wee small hours of the morning and the terrible realisation would creep through my body-'Oh my God! My foot is sticking out!' But I wouldn't make any sudden movements. One sudden rash wrong move and you could be gone. Scarcely daring to breathe, I would inch my foot slowly, oh so slowly, back in under the covers . . . bit by bit . . . back into the 'No-Go' area which was covered by the rules.

I am not ashamed to admit it. I sleep on a mattress now. A mattress on the floor-with the light on. There is not a Bogey-man in the world who could work his way around that one.

Bethlehem Was Never So Crowded

You've never seen anything like it. There are thousands of people here all pushing and shoving and trying to get into the stable. One woman says she just wants to get inside and lie down and sleep on the straw. She says that she's sleeping rough in Dublin and all she wants is a bit of heat.

Three Wise Men are protesting that they should be first because they have followed a star. But the man from Cork who hasn't had a job for six years is sending them to the back of the queue. He's telling them that they don't know how lucky they are because they have got a bit of gold. A lot of people are eyeing the gold and whispering among themselves. The Wise Men are putting it out of sight. They look very uneasy.

The war refugees are telling a group of shepherds that they're starving. They want to kill the lamb and eat it. The shepherds are shaking their heads. The lamb is a present for the infant in the stable. The refugees are muttering and moving towards the shepherds.

Three men with guns are moving up and down the queue. They are searching for a Mr. Rushdie and asking lots of questions. They say they want to kill him. Two more gunmen are wandering around searching for a Catholic. Any Catholic will do. The group of gunmen who want to shoot a Protestant have gone down into the village to knock on a few doors. A host of angels is singing about peace on earth and goodwill to all men. A woman who looks like she hasn't slept for days is shouting that she wants to get into the stable right now.

She wants to tell the infant that the barring order didn't work and she is living in a hostel with her kids and her husband was outside late last night banging on the door. Someone is telling her that she will just have to wait her turn.

She is insisting that she must get in right now because if her husband turns up and finds her here there is no way of knowing what will happen. Three little children are huddled together in the cold. One of them is holding a teddy bear.

She says it's a present for the baby Jesus. She is going to give it to Him and ask him to tell her daddy to leave her alone. She's afraid to tell anybody else because she thinks it's all her fault and nobody would believe her anyway.

The crowd is getting very restless. Snow is falling. It's bitterly cold out here. One woman is not protesting or shouting or anything. She is sitting on the ground and holding a little girl who is asleep. They are both wrapped in the folds of a coloured blanket. The woman is holding one hand out and her lips are moving — "A couple of pence and I'll say a prayer for you." She is repeating it over and over again.

The Three Wise Men are leaving. Their faces show fear. A group of young men is following them.

There are a lot of placards here. People are demanding that troops get out, others want employment, decent housing, food, clothes, education, a drink of water, sight, hearing, the use of their limbs, the safe return of their husbands, medication, a weekend at home for Christmas, respect, a bit of bread, a warm jumper.

The crowd is getting bigger. Night is drawing in. None of the people has got any place to sleep. There is no room at any of the inns. Even if there was, most of these people have not got the price of a room anyway.
A fire is lighting in the snow. The smell of wood burning. Somebody is cooking a lamb. There is no sign of the shepherds anywhere. Nobody has seen them. Nobody knows anything.